Cherries Jubilee

By Florence Theriault
Gold Horse Publishing

© 2004 Theriault's Gold Horse Publishing. All rights reserved.
No part of this book may be reproduced or utilized in any form or by any means, electronic or mechanical, including photocopying, recording, or by any information retrieval system, without permission, in writing, from the author or the publisher.

To order additional copies contact:
Dollmasters
PO Box 2319
Annapolis, MD 21404
Tel. 800-966-3655, Fax 410-571-9605
www.dollmasters.com

Design by Travis Hammond
Photography by Gerald Nelson

$49
ISBN: 1-931503-29-X
Printed in Hong Kong

1. An Exceptional and Rare Schoenhut Parade Bandwagon with Seven Bandmen and Horses
20" (51 cm) wagon, about 40" overall. A carved wooden bandwagon with wooden wheels is lavishly decorated in gilt and red paint over embossed paperboard with lavish relief scenes of horses and chariots, lion's heads, elephants, and clowns above the embossed name "Humpty Dumpty Circus". Seated upon the graduated height seats of the bandwagon are six bandmen in red felt parade uniforms with articulated bodies, some with painted moustache, each with wooden detachable parade helmet and a musical instrument, and a seventh man, the leader of the band, who sits at the front with a baton. The wagon is being pulled by four dappled Schoenhut wooden horses with original harnesses, posed upon wooden wheeled bases. Condition: very good, coats replaced except the driver. Comments: Schoenhut, circa 1910. Value Points: exceptionally rare American toy, made for a few years only, is dramatically designed to perfectly capture the essence of the real circus; few examples are known to exist. $11,000/15,000

2. Wonderful Large German Bisque Anniversary Doll, "Jubilee Googly"
23" (59 cm.) Bisque socket head, brown glass sleep and side-glancing googly eyes, dark curly lashes, dark eyeliner, feathered angled brows, accented nostrils of button nose, closed mouth with defined space between the shaded lips, dimpled chin, brunette mohair wig, composition and wooden ball-jointed toddler body with side-hip jointing, nicely costumed. Condition: generally excellent. Marks: 165-12. Comments: Hertel and Schwab for Strobel and Wilkin, the model was created in 1914 to represent the Campbell Kid; in that year Campbell Soup Co. was celebrating its 50th anniversary. Value Points: fabulous doll with intriguing history in exceptionally large size for this model, with toddler body and very choice bisque. $11,000/15,000

3. Beautiful Large French Bisque Poupee by Pierre-Francois Jumeau

25" (64 cm.) Pale pressed bisque swivel head on kid-edged bisque shoulder plate, almond-shaped pale blue glass inset eyes, dark eyeliner, painted lashes, arched feathered brows, mauve blushed eye shadow, accented nostrils, closed mouth with accented lips, separately modeled pierced ears, blonde mohair wig over cork pate. French kid gusset-jointed body with shapely waist, antique silk and velvet burgundy gown, bonnet, black leather boots, undergarments. Condition: generally excellent, finger tips worn on right hand. Comments: Pierre-Francois Jumeau, circa 1875, his classic portrait poupee model that evolved into the first model of the portrait bebe created by his son Emile Jumeau. Value Points: wonderful large size enhances the expressive dreamy-like features of the rare model, original body. $3500/4500

4. French Automaton "Little Girl with Basket of Fruit" by Leopold Lambert

20" (51 cm.) A bisque-headed girl with large blue glass paperweight eyes and closed mouth is standing upon a green velvet covered base; she has carton torso and legs, wire upper arms, bisque forearms, blonde mohair wig, cork pate, and a lavish original silk and lace ivory and burgundy costume and elaborate straw bonnet. The girl carries a fruit seller's basket filled with cherries and berries, and holds a cherry in her right hand, and a berry in her left. When keywound, music plays, the girl nods her head forward and backward, then side to side while alternately offering the fruit in each hand. Condition: generally excellent, left arm reglued under costume. Marks: Depose Tete Jumeau 4 (artist checkmarks, on head) L.B. (key). Comments: Leopold Lambert, circa 1890. Value Points: superb automaton with well-functioning appealing movements, costume and theme that complement the musical tune "Mamzelle Nitouche" (Miss Prude), listed on paper label on base. $6500/8500

5. An All-Original Gorgeous French Bisque E.J. Bebe by Emile Jumeau

18" (46 cm.) Pressed bisque socket head, very deep luminous blue glass paperweight inset eyes, dark painted eyeliner, painted lashes, mauve blushed eye shadow, arched brush-stroked and multi-feathered brows, accented nostrils, closed mouth with shaded and accented lips, separately modeled pierced ears, blonde mohair wig over cork pate. French composition and wooden fully-jointed body with straight wrists. Condition: generally excellent. Marks: Depose E 8 J (head) Jumeau Medaille d'Or Paris (body). Comments: Emile Jumeau, circa 1885, the bebe is celebrating its 120th birthday. Value Points: superb quality of bisque, splendid eyes, original body and body finish, original Jumeau couturier dress designed by Ernestine Jumeau, matching bonnet, original undergarments, socks and leather shoes signed Depose Bebe Jumeau 8. $8500/10,000

Cherries Jubilee

6. Superb French Paper Mache Poupee in Original Wedding Costume
16" (41 cm.) Paper mache shoulder head of adult woman with oval-shaped face and elegant elongated throat, small black enamel inset eyes, delicately painted lashes, arched brows, accented eye corners and nostrils of aquiline nose, blushed cheeks, closed mouth, black painted pate with center slit for insertion of original human hair wig, pink kid poupee body with slender waist, stitched and separated fingers. Condition: generally excellent. Comments: French, circa 1850. Value Points: very refined expression and pose with superb preservation of original complexion and painting, original body, wearing fine antique gown of silk organza decorated with tiny flowers, wax blossom coronet, flowers in hair, undergarments, black slippers. $2000/2500

7. French "Globe de Mariage" with Elaborate Arrangement
20" (51 cm.) With rich gilt ormolu frame having fretwork railing that encloses a velvet cushion tufted with metal gilt petals, and decorated all around with elaborately shaped ormolu flowers, leaves, four framed mirrors, dove with wreath in its beak, and porcelain flowers. Arranged around the cushion is an orange blossom wedding coronet and flowers. The arrangement is presented upon a wooden base, under blown glass dome. The presentation of a "globe de marriage" upon engagement was traditional in certain French provincial regions, particularly Normandy, throughout the early 19th century, and according to tradition, a mirror was added to the arrangement for each year of engagement. Excellent condition. Circa 1875. $600/900

8. German All-Bisque Mignonette with Original Elaborate Costume
5" (13 cm.) Bisque swivel head on kid-edged bisque torso, blue glass enamel inset eyes, painted lashes and brows, accented nostrils, closed mouth with center accent line, peg-jointed bisque arms and legs, painted white stockings with brown two-strap heeled shoes. Condition: generally excellent. Comments: circa 1890. Value Points: lovely mignonette has swivel head, closed mouth, and wears superb early ivory satin gown trimmed with crystal and pearl beading, matching cape and train. $800/1200

9. Superb French Bisque Poupee with Original Gown

17" (44 cm.) Pale bisque swivel head on kid-edged bisque shoulder plate, blue glass enamel inset eyes, painted lashes, lightly feathered brows, accented nostrils and eye corners, closed mouth with lightly accented pale lips, unpierced ears, blonde mohair wig in elaborate original coiffure over cork pate, French kid gusset-jointed fashion body with shapely waist and derriere, stitched and separated fingers. Condition: generally excellent. Comments: circa 1870. Value Points: outstanding poupee with superb bisque and painting, very sturdy original body, wearing original silk gown with rich black lace and black bead trim, extended train, detachable floor-length sash, undergarments, boots. $2500/3500

10. Five Bisque Theatre Dolls in Original Costumes

6" (15 cm.) Each has bisque shoulder head with sculpted blonde hair and painted facial features, original muslin stitch-jointed body, bisque hands and lower legs, and each is costumed elaborately to represent a member of the court, including three ladies and two gentlemen. Condition: generally excellent, one missing foot, one missing hand. Comments: circa 1880, based upon the 1877 patent of Charles Keller for "Bebe Francais", describing a costumed dollhouse type doll; a major portion of his business concerned elaborately costumed miniature theatre dolls such as this set. Value Points: wonderfully detailed costumes are well-preserved on the rare to find dolls. $600/900

Cherries Jubilee

11. A Charming German Bisque Googly, 221, by Kestner
13" (33 cm.) Bisque socket head with rounded facial modeling, large brown glass side-glancing googly eyes, dark eyeliner, lightly feathered brows, angled brows with ochre-shading, accented nostrils of button nose, closed mouth with shaded lips in smiling expression, blonde mohair wig over plaster pate, composition and wooden ball-jointed toddler body with side-hip jointing, well costumed. Condition: generally excellent. Marks: F made in Germany 10 JDK 221 Ges Gesch. Comments: Kestner, circa 1912, the model was inspired by the composition-bodied Kewpie also made by Kestner at this time. Value Points: most endearing of the googlies with gentle yet mischievous expression, choice bisque, original body and body finish. $6000/8000

12. Small Pull-Toy Lamb on Wheels
11" (26 cm.) Fleecy-lambswool-covered paper mache lamb with luxurious coat has painted hooves, shaved face, glass eyes, fancy ribbons, green wooden frame with metal wheels. When the lamb's head is tipped forward it realistically bleats. Excellent condition. Circa 1920. $700/900

13. Delightful and All-Original French Bisque Bebe
9" (23 cm.) Bisque socket head, black glass sleep eyes, painted lashes, feathered brows, accented nostrils, open mouth, four teeth, blonde mohair wig. French composition and wooden ball-jointed body. Condition: generally excellent. Marks: SFBJ 60 Paris 6/0. Comments: SFBJ, circa 1915, the doll was marketed as Bebe Mascotte according to its original box in which it is still preserved. Value Points: fine unplayed with condition, the little girl wears an elaborate antique cotton and lace dress, original undergarments, peach silk bonnet, socks and little brown leather shoes. $700/900

14. Large Rare German Bisque Character, 1488, by Simon and Halbig
28" (71 cm.) Bisque socket head, small blue glass sleep eyes, painted lashes, incised eyeliner, brushstroked and multi-feathered brows,

accented nostrils of upturned nose, closed mouth, defined space between the richly shaded lips, blonde mohair wig, composition and wooden ball-jointed body. Condition: generally excellent. Marks: 1488 Simon & Halbig 15. Comments: Simon and Halbig, circa 1915. Value Points: rare model in superb large size has exemplary bisque and modeling, fine lustrous patina of complexion, very fine antique costume comprising embroidered gingham dress, lace cap, undergarments, shoes. $5000/7500

15. *German Bisque Character, D.V. by Swaine and Co in Original Costume*

15" (38 cm.) Solid domed bisque socket head, painted blonde baby hair, small blue glass sleep eyes, painted lashes, heavily modeled eyelids, shaded brows, accented nostrils and eye corners, closed mouth with defined space between the shaded lips, composition bent limb baby body. Condition: generally excellent. Marks: D.V. 6 (incised) S & Co Ges Geschutz (green stamp). Comments: Swaine and Co. circa 1915. Value Points: especially fine quality of sculpting and quality of bisque, antique baby smock and matching panties, jacket, slippers. $800/1000

16. *Large Pull-Toy Lamb on Wheels*

16"l. (40 cm.) A paper mache and wooden lamb with luxurious woolly coat has painted hooves, shaved face, glass eyes, fancy ribbons and pull-string, blue wooden frame with metal wheels, the frame signed G.C.C. with illustration of bulldog. When the lamb's head is tipped forward it realistically bleats. Excellent condition. Circa 1920. $900/1300

17. French Doll's Armoire with Original Contents and Doll
27" armoire. 10" doll. A wooden armoire with dark walnut finish has beautifully paneled arch-shaped doors and crest, and opens to reveal an exceptionally fitted interior comprising stacks of doll-sized linens, towels, table spreads and napkins, tied in sets with original rose silk ribbons, or pinned to doors that are fitted on the interior with dotted tulle; a single drawer at the bottom contains more linens. Arranged in the center is a small bisque headed doll with blue glass eyes, open mouth, four teeth, original brunette mohair wig, five piece composition body, wearing original factory costume with bretelle-trimmed jacket, pleated bonnet with floral trim, marked AM 1896. Comments: the armoire appeared in various French department store Etrennes catalog, circa 1896, as a play model to teach young girls about a properly fitted home. Value Points: exceptionally preserved and beautifully designed armoire and contents. $2000/2500

18. German All-Bisque Brownie by Palmer Cox
8" (20 cm.) All-bisque one-piece figure of standing Brownie as Chinese Man with sculpted googly downcast eyes, sculpted costume comprising blue tunic and pants, pom-pom cap, yellow slippers with upturned toes; the detail of sculpting includes long queue down its back torso. Germany, circa 1900. Excellent condition of the rare figure designed by Palmer Cox. $500/700

19. French Bisque Miniature Character, 247, by SFBJ with Original Trousseau
7" doll. A bisque headed doll with blue glass sleep eyes, painted lashes and brows, closed mouth with painted teeth, blonde mohair wig, composition bent limb baby body, is wearing original white pique baby gown, cap and bib. Condition: generally excellent. Marks: 22 SFBJ 247 Paris 0. Comments: SFBJ, circa 1910. Value Points: the doll is presented in its original store box with paper lace edging (lid missing) containing a beautifully detailed trousseau, comprising pique baby coat, pique baby jacket, blue silk dress with lace trim, bone-handled baby rattle with blue silk ribbons, and baby bottle with blue silk ribbons, preserved in beautiful original state. $2000/2500

20. Rare German Bisque Character, 169, by Kley and Hahn in Superb Costume
22" (56 cm.) Bisque socket head, blue glass sleep eyes, dark painted curly lashes, lightly feathered brows, accented eye corners, shaded nostrils, closed mouth with shaded and accented lips, brunette mohair wig, composition and wooden ball-jointed toddler body with side-hip jointing. Condition: generally excellent. Marks: K&H (in banner) 169-10. Comments: Kley and Hahn, circa 1912. Value Points: wonderful expression on the wistful-faced pouty character, with desirable toddler body having original finish, superb antique dress, bonnet, undergarments, leather shoes. $2000/2500

21. German Bisque Toddler, 116A by Kammer and Reinhardt
21" (53 cm.) Bisque socket head, blue glass sleep eyes, painted lashes, short feathered brows, accented nostrils and eye corners, closed mouth modeled as though open with shaded and outlined lips, defined tongue and two beaded upper teeth, blonde mohair wig, composition and wooden fully-jointed toddler body with side-hip jointing, antique costume comprising dress, ruffled bonnet, undergarments, shoes and socks. Condition: generally excellent. Marks: K*R Simon & Halbig 116/A 50. Comments: Kammer and Reinhardt, circa 1915. Value Points: unusually fine detail of modeling with great definition of laughter lines and dimples, fine quality of bisque, rarer toddler body with original finish. $1200/1600

22. Very Large German Bisque Child, 79, by Heinrich Handwerck
35" (90 cm.) Bisque socket head, brown glass sleep eyes, dark eyeliner, dark painted lashes, slightly modeled brush-stoked and feathered brows, accented eye corners and nostrils, open mouth, shaded and accented lips, four porcelain teeth, pierced ears, blonde mohair wig, composition and wooden ball-jointed body, antique costume. Condition: generally excellent. Marks: 79 17 1/2 Germany Halbig (head) Handwerck 8 (body). Comments: Heinrich Handwerck, circa 1890. Value Points: beautiful large size doll with choice bisque, original body and body finish, enhanced by rare extended-length mohair wig extending nearly to her waist. $1200/1500

23. French Child's Toilette Set with Kate Greenaway Type Illustrations
19" (48 cm.) A wooden framed dressing table with double towel bars and cabinet has fitted creamware faience table top and seven matching faience toiletry dishes, each decorated with delicate pastel drawings of children in the romantic Kate Greenaway style; a variety of different scenes are shown. Included is divided washbowl with handle, water pitcher, two round jars with lids, chamberpot, and two smaller pitchers (one with lid). Each piece is signed Sarreguimine. Excellent condition. French, circa 1890. A beautifully decorated set with lavish

appointments and fine original condition. $1200/1500

24. Rare German All-Bisque Doll
8 1/2" (22 cm.) Bisque swivel head on kid-edged bisque torso with defined musculature detail, brown glass inset eyes, dark painted eyeliner, rose blushed eye shadow and cheek and chin blush, painted lashes and brows, accented nostrils and eye corners, open mouth, two upper and one lower square cut teeth, pierced ears, blonde mohair wig, peg-jointed bisque arms and legs with detailed musculature and pose, painted knee-high orange stockings, black high laced and heeled boots, antique dress. Condition: generally excellent, tiny flake at right stringing hole of shoulder. Comments: Germany, circa 1885. Value Points: very sought-after mignonette model with wonderfully detail body, her plump dimpled legs descending to very shapely ankles, blushing detailing the creases and dimples of arms. $2000/2500

25. German Bisque Child, 241, by Kestner Known as "Hilda's Older Sister"
25" (64 cm.) Bisque socket head, blue glass sleep eyes, dark eyeliner, painted lashes, short feathered brows, accented nostrils and eye corners, open mouth, shaded and accented lips, four porcelain teeth, impressed dimples at lip corners, blonde mohair wig, composition and wooden ball-jointed body. Condition: generally excellent. Marks: K made in Germany 14 JDK 241 (head) Germany (body). Comments: Kestner, circa 1915, the model appears as an older child version of Hilda, but is much more rarely found. Value Points: elusive and lovely character doll with finest quality of bisque and painting, original signed body and body finish, fine antique costume comprising dress, undergarments, stockings, shoes, bonnet. $2500/3500

26. Very Rare German Bisque Character "Moritz" by Kammer and Reinhardt
16" (40 cm.) Bisque socket head with chubby and dimpled facial modeling, small brown glass flirty eyes, long painted lashes, modeled brows with decorative glaze, upturned nose with accented nostrils, closed mouth in beaming smile with shaded and outlined lips, impressed cheek dimples, auburn human hair, composition and wooden fully jointed body with painted white socks and brown shoes, antique woolen suit. Condition: generally excellent. Comments: "Moritz", by Kammer and Reinhardt, circa 1914, based upon the original illustration in the books of German author Wilhelm Busch. Value Points: very rare model with choice bisque, original flirty eyes, original body uniquely designed for this doll only. $10,000/14,000

Cherries Jubilee

27. Very Rare American Carved Wooden Exhibition Horse by Schoenhut
29" (74 cm.) An all-wooden carved horse with brown glass eyes, carved nostrils and open mouth with defined teeth, carved detail of knees and hooves, horsehair mane and tail, leather ear, is mounted upon a wheeled wooden platform with center iron rod in the manner of a carousel. The horse is painted in the dappled style of the classic Schoenhut circus horse with ochre shading at the nose and black hooves. Condition: structurally excellent, fine professional restoration of painting. Comments: Schoenhut, circa 1910, the horse was created as an exhibition model for display presentation. Value Points: extremely rare, very few examples of this exhibition model are known to exist. $3000/4000

27A. German Mohair St. Bernard on Wheels by Steiff
14"l. (35 cm.) Excelsior-filled champagne-colored mohair St. Bernard with brown glass eyes, floppy ears, brown embroidered nose, brown leather collar with bell and chain link to original leather leash, and mounted upon a cast iron frame with spoked iron wheels. With original Steiff button in ear. Germany, Steiff, circa 1915. $900/1300

28. A Beautiful Wooden Character Doll, Model 308, by Schoenhut
19" (48 cm.) Carved/pressed wooden socket head, intaglio carved light brown eyes with prominent black pupils and white eye dots, brown upper eyeliner, lightly feathered brows, accented nostrils, closed mouth with pensive expression, brunette mohair wig, wooden spring-jointed body with holes in feet for positioning. Condition: generally excellent, small nose rub. Marks: Schoenhut Doll, Pat. Jan 17, '11, USA & Foreign Countries. Comments: Schoenhut, circa 1914, model 308. Value Points: rarer model with superb expression, original finish, antique whitewear dress may be original, undergarments, shoes stockings. $900/1200

28A. Rare Carved Wooden Pouty Character Doll, Model 304, by Schoenhut
16" (43 cm.) Carved/pressed wooden socket head, intaglio carved painted blue eyes with black pupils and white eye dots, incised upper eyeliner, lightly feathered brows, accented nostrils of rounded nose, closed mouth with pensive expression, brunette mohair wig, wooden spring-jointed body with holes in feet for positioning. Condition: generally excellent, small nose rub. Marks: Schoenhut Doll, Pat. Jan 17, '11, USA & Foreign Countries. Comments: Schoenhut, circa 1914, model 304, the Schoenhut version of K*R 114 character doll. Value Points: very rare model with most endearing expression, original finish, antique white wear dress may be original, undergarments, woven straw bonnet, shoes stockings. $900/1200

29. Rare American Wooden Character Doll, 102, by Schoenhut with Carved Hair
16" (41 cm.) Carved wooden socket head, carved brown hair with braided style held by a pink bow at the back of thread, brown intaglio carved eyes, prominent black pupils, white eyedots, black upper eyeliner, shaded nostrils, closed mouth, all-wooden carved body with spring-jointing, holes in feet for positioning. Condition: generally excellent, small nose rub. Marks: Schoenhut Doll. Pat. Jan 17. '11. USA & Foreign Countries. Comments: Schoenhut, circa 1914, model 102. Value Points: rare carved hair girl has fine original finish with lustrous patina, antique dress is probably original Schoenhut, undergarments, original Schoenhut ankle boots. $2000/2500

30. Wonderful German Bisque Character, 520, by Kley and Hahn in Rare Large Size
29" (74 cm.) Bisque socket head, painted facial features, large brown shaded eyes with artistic outline, white eye dots, thick black upper eyeliner with short fringed lashes, red upper eyeliner, short feathered brows, accented nostrils and eye corners, closed mouth with outlined lips, brunette human hair in long curls, composition and wooden ball-jointed body. Condition: generally excellent. Marks: K&H (in banner) 520 14. Comments: Kley and Hahn, circa 1910, from their art character series. Value Points: wonderful expression and quality of bisque on the rare character series, its rarity quite enhanced by the unusually large size. $7500/9500

Cherries Jubilee

31. French Bisque Poupee by Jumeau with Original Costume
16" (42 cm.) Bisque swivel head on kid-edged bisque shoulder plate, large blue glass enamel inset eyes with spiral threading, lightly painted lashes, brush-stroked brows, accented nostrils and eye corners, closed mouth with outlined lips, pierced ears, blonde mohair wig in original elaborate coiffure with maroon ribbons, kid fashion body with gusset jointing, shapely waist, stitched and separated fingers. Condition: generally excellent. Marks: 6. Comments: Jumeau, circa 1875, the poupee model with larger eye sockets evolved into the first facial model of bebe by Jumeau, and is historically important for that purpose. Value Points: beautiful poupee with original wig, choice bisque, wearing original blue and white plaid two-piece gown with delicate trim, undergarments, leather shoes. $2500/3500

32. French Bisque Portrait Poupee by Jumeau
17" (45 cm.) Pale bisque swivel head on kid-edged bisque shoulder plate, almond-shaped blue glass enamel inset eyes, dark eyeliner, painted lashes, mauve blushed eye shadow, arched feathered brows, accented nostrils and eye corners, closed mouth with accented lips, pierced ears, blonde mohair wig over cork pate, kid fashion body with gusset jointing, shapely waist, stitched and separated fingers. Condition: generally excellent. Marks: 4. (head and shoulders). Comments: Pierre-Francois Jumeau, circa 1875. Value Points: gorgeous portrait lady with most delicate bisque and painting, original body, original costume in patterned blue and cream cotton, straw bonnet, undergarments, shoes. $2500/3500

33. Superb French Bisque Poupee "Lily" by Madame Lavallee-Peronne
17" (45 cm.) Bisque swivel head on kid-edged bisque shoulder plate, blue glass enamel inset eyes, dark eyeliner, painted lashes, arched brows, accented nostrils and eye corners, closed mouth with accented lips, pierced ears, brunette mohair wig over cork pate. French wooden poupee body with dowel-jointing at shoulders, elbows, wrists, hips, knees and ankles, swivel waist. Condition: generally excellent. Marks: A La Poupee de Nuremberg 21 rue de Choiseul, Lavalle-Peronne Trousseau Complets Reparations Paris (paper label on torso). Comments: Madame Lavalle-Peronne, of the prestigious doll shop A La Poupee de Nuremberg, circa 1865, the doll was introduced as "Lily" in the doll journal La Poupee Modele that she edited, and patterns appeared in the journal designed to fit this doll. Value Points: very rare doll in superb original condition, with flawless original finish on body, extra body articulations, original label, choice bisque, included is the fine miniature wooden chair in which she is seated, and her antique undergarments. $7500/9500

34. Rare French Bisque Miniature Bebe by Jumeau
9" (23 cm.) Pressed bisque socket head with very pale bisque, pale blue glass enamel inset eyes with spiral threading, dark eyeliner, lightly feathered brows, accented nostrils and eye corners, closed mouth with slightly smiling expression, accented lips, auburn mohair wig over cork pate, French composition and wooden fully-jointed body, straight wrists. Condition: generally excellent. Marks: N 1 (head) Jumeau Medaille d'Or Paris (body). Comments: Emile Jumeau, one of the first bebes offered by the firm, circa 1878. Value Points: the very rare "N" model, only appearing in this tiny size and with smiling expression, has most endearing air, original signed body, original dress, antique shoes, bonnet and undergarments; few examples are known to exist. $6000/9000

Cherries Jubilee

35. An Extraordinary French Bisque Bebe "Blondine" with Trousseau and Provenance

22" (56 cm.) Bisque head with solid dome, blue glass paperweight inset eyes, dark eyeliner, painted lashes, brush-stroked and feathered brows, rose blushed eye shadow, accented eye corners and nostrils, slightly parted lips with delicate accent lines, row of tiny porcelain teeth, pierced ears, original blonde lambswool wig, carton torso with clockwork mechanism, composition arms, hinged hips with kid cover, composition lower legs, keywind mechanism in torso that causes doll to cry mama and wave arms and legs. Condition: generally excellent. Comments: doll by Jules Steiner, circa 1885. Value Points: in pristine unplayed with condition, as though never removed from her original box that is labeled in pencil script "Blondine", the remarkable bebe owns an extraordinary trousseau, some stored in a fine ebony black trunk with leather straps and brass hardware, and other clothing stored in original boxes. The clothing, that is as crisp and pristine as the day it was made, comprises: *Silk velvet winter coat with white boa trim and matching bonnet with seed pearl clusters and tiny feathers trimmed with glass beads, maroon stockings, and black velvet shoes with silver buckles. (being worn by Blondine); 5 additional very elaborate silk and woolen dresses, one with matching muff; 11 additional chapeaux of extraordinary detail and design; 3 fine lace bonnets; 8 knit caps; 12 pairs of stockings; 5 bibs or shawls; 8 night sacs or blouses; 5 pantalets; 6 petticoats; 8 chemises (7 initialed "B"); Blue woolen baby dress; Elaborate Christening gown; Blue tricot dress with matching hood and slippers; 4 additional pairs of shoes (3 signed B.V. for Brasseur-Videlier, the prestige Paris doll shop); Accessories including 2 curved combs (possibly made by the Convert family), other decorative combs, (some in box from A La Tentation, another prestige Paris doll shop) fine jewelry, bone rattle, jump robe, two boxes Bapteme de ma Poupee, and blown glass decanter and glasses in original box.* $30,000/55,000

Photographs of the doll and elements of her trousseau are shown on these and the following two pages.

Cherries Jubilee

The Story of Blondine

Blondine and her trousseau originated from the French estate of the Convert family of Oyonnax in the Jura Mountains. Beginning about 1860 the Convert name became important in the production of beautiful hair combs from the newly invented material of celluloid. Although wooden decorative combs had been produced in the town for more than a century from the plentiful nearly mountain woods, this new material allowed a level of abundance that had not existed before. The Convert family thrived and enjoyed the fruits of their prosperity for themselves, and, presumably, their daughter. Introduced in Paris at that time was the new doll phenomenon know as "bebe"; its originator was Jules Steiner to whom they felt an affinity as he had been born in Dijon, not very far from their own home town. So on a far-away trip to Paris, some 500 kms from Oyonnaz, the Convert family chose a Bebe Steiner for their daughter, and on subsequent visits to prestigious Parisian doll shops they added a trousseau for that doll that was notable in its luxury. The doll was named Blondine, its still-faint name handwritten on the box in which it has been store for more than 135 years. The name of the daughter is not known nor is the reason why the doll and its trousseau remained unplayed with, still preserved today in unimaginably pristine condition.

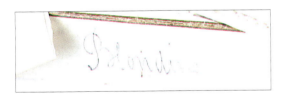

Cherries Jubilee

36. German Bisque Pouty, 7246, by Gebruder Heubach
26" (66 cm.) Pink-tinted bisque socket head, blue glass sleep eyes, painted lashes, dark eyeliner, brushstroked and feathered brows, accented eye corners and nostrils, closed mouth with accented lips, brunette mohair wig, composition and wooden ball-jointed body. Condition: generally excellent, some body repaint. Marks: 7246 Heubach (sunburst) Germany. Comments: Gebruder Heubach, circa 1912. Value Points: most appealing wistful expression is artfully achieved, enhanced by very fine antique costume of 1912 era boy. $1200/1700

37. Large German Bisque Pouty, 7246 by Gebruder Heubach
28" (71 cm.) Pink-tinted bisque socket head, brown glass sleep eyes, dark eyeliner, painted lashes, brushstroked and fringed brows, accented eye corners and nostrils, closed mouth with downcast pouty lips, accent line between the lips, brunette mohair wig, composition and wooden ball-jointed body. Condition: generally excellent, small restoration on left bottom eye rim. Marks: 7246 11 Heubach (sunburst mark) Germany. Comments: Gebruder Heubach, circa 1912. Value Points: rare model in wonderful large size, excellent quality of bisque with lustrous patina, wonderful antique costume of young boy of the 1912 era. $1200/1800

38. Extremely Rare Schoenhut Wooden Teddy Roosevelt on Safari
8" (20 cm.) Comprising portrait figure of Teddy Roosevelt with painted hair and facial features including spectacles and drooping moustache to depict the 26th president, wooden body with articulation at shoulders, elbows, hips and knees and separately defined thumbs, wearing original khaki uniform with belt, ammunition box, gun and rifle, painted brown stockings and brown shoes, and having yellow wooden cap; along with brown-complexioned Native Guide with musculature carved torso, leather ears, wearing original printed cotton pants; and with ten animals, viz: alligator with glass eyes (one flipper replaced); Arabian one-humped camel with glass eyes and closed mouth; giraffe with painted eyes and carved open mouth; leopard with glass eyes and open mouth; lion with cloth mane, ball-jointed neck, glass eyes and open mouth; style III ostrich; rhinoceros with glass eyes and horn; tiger with glass eyes and open mouth; zebra with glass eyes and closed mouth; and zebu with glass eyes. Condition: very good to excellent throughout. Teddy has paint flakes on back of hair (under cap). Comments: the Teddy Roosevelt Safari Set was introduced by Schoenhut in December 1909; in her book Under the Big Top, Evelyn Ackerman described the Teddy Roosevelt figure as "having a superb likeness ...without resorting to a comic, cartoon-like characterization." Value Points: exceptionally rare Schoenhut ensemble group includes many rare animals from their first production period. $9000/14,000

Cherries Jubilee

Cherries Jubilee

39. *Very Rare Schoenhut Side Show Parade Wagon with Horses*
20" (50 cm) wagon. 32" (81 cm) overall. A wooden parade flatbed wagon with stage top is lavishly decorated with embossed paperboard on the sides having richly gilded circus scenes including chariot rider with horse, lion head, and bareback rider, and is labeled with raised letters "Humpty Dumpty Circus". The flatbed was decorated wooden wheels, driver's seat with clown driver, chained posts around the perimeter, and is driven by a team of dappled horses with harnesses on wooden wheeled base. Standing upon the wagon, as though on exhibit, are three characters, each with overscaled paper mache head having intricate details of painting and accessories such as spectacles and cap, and classic Schoenhut clown body, comprising Foxy Grandpa, Jockey, and Baby. Condition: good to very good, base of horses replaced, one chain post missing, two chain posts replaced, some overall dustiness and flakes to paint on back of baby head, minor face touch-up on grandpa and jockey. Comments: Schoenhut, circa 1910 from their series of four circus wagons, made for a very few years, with all of the original characters and superb and imaginative design. $8000/11,000

Cherries Jubilee

40. Two Wooden Comic Characters by Schoenhut

9" (including hats). Each has carved/pressed wooden head with gesso and painted finish to depict caricature model as portrayed in comic strip series. Boob McNutt with thick red hair, down-glancing O-shaped eyes, small wooden hat at top of head, all wooden body with over-sized feet, jointing at shoulders and hips; and Happy Hooligan with red tin can wooden hat perched at top of bald pate, googly-painted eyes, over-sized ears, elongated skinny neck, over-sized feet, jointing at shoulders and hips. Condition: generally excellent. Marks: copyright 1924 International Features Service, Pat. Applied For (paper label on one). Comments: Schoenhut, circa 1915. Value Points: very rare characters by Schoenhut with wonderfully expressed character features, original accessories and original cloth costumes. $1200/1800

41. "Farmer and Milkmaid" by Schoenhut

8" Farmer. Carved wooden figures depict a smiling-face Farmer with painted goatee and brows, painted tall black boots; along with milkmaid having smiling expression, brown sculpted hair, blue stockings and black shoes; with four farm animals, viz: cow with glass eyes, closed mouth, bell; pig with glass eyes and carved open mouth; cat with glass eyes, whiskers, tail and closed mouth; and rabbit with glass eyes and closed mouth. Condition: very good to excellent. Comments: Schoenhut, circa 1912. Value Points: wonderfully detailed early version of the Americana set, the Farmer and milkmaid each wearing original costumes, and having original milk pail and stool. $1500/2200

42. "Mary and Her Lamb" by Schoenhut

8" Mary. Carved wooden figure of young girl with sculpted hair, painted face with somber expression, jointing at shoulders and hips, painted blue stockings and black over-sized feet, wearing original factory costume and straw hat; along with glass-eyed lamb with carved wooden tail, bell around the neck. Condition: generally excellent.

Comments: Schoenhut, the first series introduced by Schoenhut in 1908. Value Points: rare set in wonderfully preserved condition. $1200/1500

Cherries Jubilee

43. Six Schoenhut Carved Circus Animals
Each about 8". Each is carved wood with realistic detailing of the animal features and posturing; including polar bear with glass eyes and carved open mouth; poodle with cloth ruff, glass eyes and open mouth; sea lion with glass eyes and open mouth; goat with glass eyes and leather beard, ears, horns and tail; kangaroo with glass eyes; and Style I monkey with white face, silk hat and elongated legs. Condition: very good to excellent throughout. Comments: Schoenhut, circa 1910. Value Points: six early period animals with superb detail of carving and well-preserved original finish. $1800/2300

44. Rare Schoenhut Chariot with Clown and Burro
16" (41 cm) overall. A red wooden framed chariot with pressed paperboard sides decorated with embossed winged and scroll designs centered by a lion's head at the front has two wooden wheels with carved designs, and is being pulled by a carved wooden burro with glass eyes and original harness. Standing in the chariot is a carved wooden clown with two-part head, original costume with clover, diamond and star designs. Condition: very good, all painting and parts appear original, separation at side seams of head. Comments: Schoenhut, circa 1905, from their series of four circus wagons. Value Points: the chariot and clown combines great rarity and imaginative design; few examples are known to exist. $2000/3000

45. American Brown-Complexioned Bonneted Mystery Child Attributed to Leo Moss
16" (41 cm.) Brown-complexioned wax-over-composition socket head with sculpted ribbed stocking cap edged by tight curls at forehead and sides of head, brown glass inset eyes, heavy modeled eyelids, black brows with sculpting detail, accented nostrils, closed mouth with accent line between the lips, brown composition ball-jointed body, wearing brown flannel coat with embroidered collar and cuffs, maroon cotton dress, undergarments, stockings, boots. Condition: generally excellent. Comments: attributed to Leo Moss, the black itinerant artist is believed to have worked in Georgia in the early 20th century, creating black portrait dolls from gathered scraps that he carefully saved from his occasional work in house painting and wall-papering; the attribution is uncertain. Value Points: the mystery doll, indubitably of American folk art origins, is superb, with artistic details of sculpted facial expression, cap and hair, enhanced by fine lustrous patina. $2000/2500

46. American Black Portrait Doll "Leotta" Attributed to Leo Moss
22" (56 cm.) Black paper mache composition head with tightly curled sculpted black curls, large brown glass inset eyes, heavy eyelids, thick black sculpted brows in furrowed expression, broad nose with accented nostrils, closed mouth with downcast pouty lips, three sculpted tears, muslin torso, disc-jointed brown composition arms and legs, cotton muslin dress with smocking detail, undergarments, black stockings, shoes. Condition: generally excellent. Marks: L.M. (shoulder plate) Leotta 2 years 1920 (handwritten, handstitched tag on front torso). Comments: attributed to Georgia artist. Leo Moss, circa 1920; the child with tears is believed to have been a tribute to the young daughter of Moss. Value Points: superb artistry of the soulful-faced child with most appealing characterization, fine original condition, intriguing mystery of paper label. $3000/4000

47. Three Poured Wax Black Portrait Dolls by Vargas
each about 7" (17 cm.) Each of three figures depicting adult black person is of poured wax with highly characterized features, tiny glass bead eyes, sculpted hair, body posed in unique manner, attached to original wooden base. Each doll is wearing imaginative cotton costume that is lightly wax-dipped to hold its position, and accessories appropriate to the doll are included. Condition: generally excellent, few finger tips missing. Marks: Harriet's 318 Royal Street New Orleans, La. (paper label on base of man). Comments: the wax miniature portrait dolls were made by the Vargas family of New Orleans in the early 20th century. Value Points: superb detail of artistry on the rarely found American figures. $800/1000

Cherries Jubilee

48. German Bisque Googly, 221, by Kestner
11" (28 cm.) Bisque socket head with rounded facial modeling, large round blue glass side-glancing googly eyes, painted lashes, brown arched brows with ochre shading, accented nostrils of pug nose, closed mouth with watermelon-slice shape, shaded lips, brunette mohair wig over plaster pate, composition and wooden ball-jointed toddler body with side-hip jointing and chubby tummy. Condition: generally excellent. Marks: C made in Germany 7 JDK 221 Ges Gesch. Comments: Kestner, circa 1912, their googly model inspired by the Kewpie. Value Points: wonderful small size of the wide-eyed googly has original wig, pate, body, body finish, and wears original knit romper suit with original label "three-piece suit, Pat. Mar.5, 1912". $5000/7500

49. Pair, Wooden Mickey and Minnie Mouse
4" (10 cm.) Each is all-wooden, swivel head, painted mask face, pie-shaped eyes, leather ears, red wooden cap, leather ears, flexible arms and legs, painted yellow gloved hands, over-sized feet, painted torsos to suggest costumes. Condition: generally excellent. Marks: Reg. US Pat. Off. Minnie Mouse. C. Walt Disney (paper label). Comments: circa 1935. Value Points: delightful miniature renditions of the comic characters. $400/500

50. Pair, Composition Dolly Dingle and Bobby Blake by Grace Drayton
9" and 10" (23 and 26 cm.) Each is all hard-composition doll with swivel head, jointed arms, one piece body and legs in posed walking position, with sculpted hair in classic style, she with topknot and short bobbed curls, he with side-parted bobbed hair, each with glass googly eyes glancing at each other, chubby dimpled cheeks, each with sculpted painted costumes. Condition: generally excellent. Comments: made in Japan for Ideal, circa 1916 according to early research by Gladys Hollander (reference attached); an identical set had an original paper label marked Ideal with Japanese lettering. Value Points: extremely rare set of googlies in wonderfully preserved condition. $2000/2500

51. Pair, Toto and Tata, Designed by Poulbot for Roullet et Decamps
14" (36 cm.) Each has paper mache head with painted facial features depicting wide-beaming smiling boy and girl, highly blushed cheeks, he with brown eyes and black fleecy hair, she with blue upper-glancing eyes and brunette hair, each with five piece composition body containing clockwork mechanism. Condition: generally excellent. Comments: Roullet and Decamps, the dolls named Toto and Tata were designed by Poulbot for Roullet et Decamps to use with this pair of mechanical dolls; when wound, the dolls sway back and forth, in an amusing manner. Value Points: rare dolls with fine original finish, well-functioning, original costumes, designed by French illustrator Poulbot. $1200/1800

52. German Brown-Complexioned Bisque Doll, 949, by Simon & Halbig
19" (48 cm.) Brown-complexioned bisque socket head, large brown glass sleep eyes, dark painted lashes, black brush-stroked brows, accented eye corners and nostrils, open mouth, shaded lips, four porcelain teeth, pierced ears, black mohair wig, brown composition and wooden ball-jointed body. Condition: generally excellent. Marks: S&H 949. Comments: Simon and Halbig, circa 1895. Value Points: rare model with very beautiful complexion, original body finish, lovely antique costume. $2000/2500

Cherries Jubilee

53. French Bisque Bebe Steiner, Figure A
28" (71 cm.) Bisque socket head, large dark blue glass paperweight inset eyes, dark painted lashes, rose blushed eye shadow, fringed eye brows, accented eye corners and shaded nostrils, closed mouth, shaded and accented lips, pierced ears, brunette human hair, Steiner composition and wooden fully-jointed body. Condition: generally excellent, arms repainted. Marks: A 19. Comments: Jules Steiner, circa 1890. Value Points: very pretty child with fine luminous bisque enhancing the large eyes and beautiful eye painting, original body. $3800/4500

54. Stunning French Bisque Bebe, Series C, in Large Size
33" (84 cm.) Bisque socket head with rounded facial modeling and plump cheeks, dramatic large blue glass paperweight inset eyes, dark eyeliner, painted lashes, brush-stroked and multi-feathered brows, accented eye corners, shaded nostrils, closed mouth with shaded and outlined lips, dimpled chin, pierced ears, Steiner composition fully jointed body. Condition: generally excellent. Marks: J. Steiner Bte SGDG Sie C. 7 Bourgoin. Comments: Jules Steiner, Series C, circa 1884. Value Points: spectacular large model of the C series bebe, with superb bisque and luminous eyes, original body and body finish, lavish antique silk and lace dress, luxe bonnet, undergarments, shoes and socks. $8500/10,500

55. French Bisque Bebe Steiner, Series C, with Deposed Sleep Eyes
18" (46 cm.) Bisque socket head, dark blue glass sleep eyes that operate from deposed system of wire lever at back of head, painted lashes, rose blushed eye shadow, brush-stroked and feathered brows, accented eye corners and nostrils, slightly parted lips with shaded and accented details, two rows of tiny teeth, blonde mohair wig. Steiner composition fully-jointed body, well costumed. Condition: generally excellent. Marks: Sie C 2 (incised on head) J. Steiner Bte SGDG J. Bourgoin St (script) Steiner 2 Bte SGDG (eyes). Comments: Jules Steiner, circa 1885. Value Points: wonderful early model of Bebe Steiner has original body, body finish, eyes, patented eye mechanism. $4000/5000

56. Rare Early French Toy Rocking Goat with Bellows
27" (68 cm.) A firm-bodied goat with brown and white fur covered body and flannel-covered head has glass inset eyes, horns, wooden legs with black hooves, red harness, and is mounted upon an elaborate iron frame that converts to rocking or wheeled shape, and has rod that causes the goat to bleat when rocked back and forth. French, circa 1870, the goat form is rare to find, this example on elaborate early frame. $2000/2500

57. French Mechanical Toy "Boy Pulling Girl on Cart" by Roullet et Decamps
14"l. 12"h. A bisque-headed boy with blue glass eyes, open mouth, four teeth, blonde mohair wig, wire upper arms, carton torso and one-piece legs, bisque hands, is pulling a wooden cart with metal wheels on which is seated a bisque-headed girl with brown glass eyes, open mouth, blonde mohair wig. Condition: generally excellent. Marks: 1078 Halbig S&H Germany (dolls). Comments: Roullet et Decamps, circa 1910, when wound the boy "walks", pulling the cart, the little girl bounces up and down and waves the whip she is holding. Value Points: amusing mechanism in beautifully preserved condition, each in original silk costumes, even with original mohair lashes. $2500/3500

Cherries Jubilee

58. An Outstanding and All-Original French Bisque Bebe Jumeau
33" (84 cm.) Bisque socket head with very deeply defined facial features, dark blue glass paperweight inset eyes, thick dark eyeliner, painted lashes, widely arched brush-stroked and multi-feathered brows, accented eye corners, shaded nostrils, closed mouth with shaded and outlined lips, impressed dimple on chin and lip corners, separately modeled and pierced ears, blonde mohair wig over cork pate. French composition and wooden fully-jointed body. Condition: generally excellent. Marks: Depose Tete Jumeau Bte SGDG 16 (head) Bebe Jumeau Diplome d'Honneur (body). Comments: Emile Jumeau, circa 1886. Value Points: A rare to find large size 16 bebe with outstanding beauty, finest sculpting and bisque, in perfectly preserved pristine condition, original wig with ribbons, earrings, crisp chemise with burgundy ribbons and trim, Bebe Jumeau gold banner, and preserved in her original labeled Jumeau box. $12,000/15,000

59. Superb French Bisque Bebe Bru by Leon Casimir Bru, Size 11
28" (71 cm.) Pressed bisque swivel head on kid-edged bisque shoulder plate with modeled breasts and shoulderblades, dramatic blue glass paperweight inset eyes, thick dark eyeliner, painted lashes, rose blushed eye shadow, brush-stroked and multi-feathered brows, accented eye corners, shaded nostrils, closed mouth with shaded, outlined lips, dimpled chin and lip corners, pierced ears, blonde mohair wig over cork pate. French kid body with slender torso, kid-over-wooden upper arms, bisque forearms. Chevrot style legs with hinged joints at hips, wooden lower legs, beautifully costumed in vintage dress of antique velvets and silk, undergarments, straw bonnet with lavish trim, leather shoes signed Bru Jne Paris. Condition: generally excellent. Marks: Bru Jne 11 (head) Bru Jne (left shoulder) 11 (right shoulder) (original paper label on chest). Comments: Leon Casimir Bru, circa 1885. Value Points: superb model of the classic bebe with exemplary bisque and painting, luminous eyes, original body in choice condition, beautiful bisque hands, lavish costume including elaborately layered undergarments and signed Bru shoes. $20,000/26,000

Cherries Jubilee

60. French Pull-Toy Burro on Wheels
19" (48 cm.) Firm-shaped burro with curly wool cover, painted face with brown glass inset eyes, carved mouth, painted legs with black hooves, leather ears, brown leather harness and saddle, brass harness trim, silver stirrup, tiny wheels under the feet, hidden wire on underbelly which causes burro to cry when pulled (cries faintly). Very good condition. French, circa 1885, a rare animal toy with detailed fittings. $900/1200

61. Rare German Bisque Character, 220, by Kestner
20" (51 cm.) Bisque socket head, blue glass sleep eyes, painted curly lashes, incised eyeliner, short stroke brows, accented nostrils and eye corners, open mouth, shaded and outlined lips, two porcelain upper teeth, blonde fleeced wig over plaster pate, composition and wooden ball-jointed toddler body with side-hip jointing, antique romper costume. Condition: generally excellent, some retouch on body finish. Marks: K made in Germany 14 JDK 220. Comments: Kestner, circa 1915. Value Points: very rare character model enhanced by deeply sculpted features and fine oily patina of bisque, original toddler body. $2500/3500

61A. German Bisque Character, 7407, by Gebruder Heubach
17" (45 cm.) Pink tinted bisque socket head, small blue glass sleep eyes, painted lashes, fringed brows, accented eye corners and nostrils, closed mouth with beautifully-shaped dimpled full lips, accent line between the lips, blonde mohair wig, composition and wooden ball-jointed body, antique costume. Condition: generally excellent. Marks: 7407 Germany 7. Comments: Gebruder Heubach, circa 1912. Value Points: rare character model with most endearing expression, lovely bisque, original body finish. $1700/2300

62. Five French All-Bisque Dolls in Original Costumes
2 1/2" (6 cm.) Each has bisque swivel head with loop attachment to bisque torso, peg-jointed bisque arms and legs, painted blue boots, painted facial features, mohair wig, and costumed in original factory costume to represent region of France. Condition: generally excellent. Comments: circa 1890, the dolls were marketed as "Lilliputians". Value Points: included are rare models representing Normandy, and brown bisque child of Martinique, all presented in original glass-front box. $500/800

63. German Bisque Character, 6970, by Gebruder Heubach
16" (41 cm.) Pink tinted bisque socket head, tiny blue glass sleep eyes, painted lashes, fringed brows, accented nostrils, closed mouth, double chin and plump cheeks, blonde mohair wig, composition and wooden ball-jointed body. Condition: generally excellent. Marks: 6970 Heubach (sunburst mark) Germany. Comments: Gebruder Heubach, circa 1915. Value Points: rare model with wonderfully detailed wistful expression, lovely bisque, original wig and antique costume. $2000/2500

64. French Presentation All-Bisque School Girl
3 1/2" doll. German all-bisque doll with sculpted bobbed hair, painted facial features, peg-jointed bisque arms and legs, blue painted shoes, is presented in an original box with decorative paper cover depicting French school girls on the path to school; inside the box are a number of miniature school accessories including valise, blackboard, ruler, journals, and such. For the French market, circa 1920. Excellent unplayed with condition. $400/500

65. Very Rare German Bisque Character by Gebruder Heubach
25" (64 cm.) Bisque socket head, blue glass sleep eyes, dark painted eyeliner, painted lashes, short brush-stroked brows, accented nostrils and eye corners, closed mouth with defined space between the shaded and outlined lips, blonde mohair wig, composition and wooden ball-jointed body, antique costume, undergarments, shoes, striped knit stockings. Condition: generally excellent. Marks: 10 Heubach (in square) Germany. Comments: Gebruder Heubach, circa 1915. Value Points: rare character model with very choice bisque, wonderfully sculpted features highlighted by prominent impressed cheek dimples. $4000/6000

Cherries Jubilee

Cherries Jubilee

66. Studio Portrait Boy by Sasha Morgenthaler in Signed Sasha Costume
20" (50 cm.) Socket head and body of synthetic material, square-shaped face with full cheeks, tiny nose, small brown painted eyes with thick black upper eyeliner and fringed lashes, short stroke brows, brunette human hair, jointing at shoulders and hips, cupped left hand. Condition: generally excellent. Marks: 90/155 Sasha (left foot) (Sasha wrist tag, and another paper tag labeled Schweitzer Heimatwerk 171 on one side and 49/155 on the other). Comments: Sasha Morgenthaler, model CI, 1955. Value points: most compelling wistful expression, the little boy wears original shirt and pants tagged Sasha, original shoes and socks, knit underwear. $4000/5000

67. Studio Portrait Girl with Braids, CIII, by Sasha Morgenthaler
20" (50 cm.) Socket head and body of synthetic material, oval face with slender throat, pronounced sculpting of nose, brown painted eyes with thick black upper eye liner enhanced by fringed lashes, arched brows, brunette human hair braids, jointing at shoulders and hips, cupped left hand. Condition: generally excellent, dent at lower left leg. Comments: Sasha Morgenthaler, model CIII, circa 1960's. Value Points: superb expression and painting on the dear child, wearing Sasha style cotton dress and undergarments, included is early (very frail) plaid woolen Sasha dress. $4000/5000

68. Studio Portrait Girl, CI, by Sasha Morgenthaler with Unique Complexion
20" (50 cm.) Socket head and body of synthetic material with unusual honey-tinted complexion and lustrous patina, square-shaped face with full cheeks, small nose, shaded blue eyes with black and white eye shadow, white dots at eye corners, brown hair with blonde highlights, jointing at shoulder and hips, cupped left hand. Condition: generally excellent. Marks: Sasha M 84/072 CI (left foot). Comments: Sasha Morgenthaler, model CI, made in 1972. Value Points: rare model with superb expression and complexion, wearing embroidered linen dress (untagged) that may be original, original knit panties, leather shoes, socks, with original wrist tag. $4000/5000

69. Brown-Complexioned Studio Toddler, F Bebe, by Sasha Morgenthaler
14" (35 cm.) Socket head and body of synthetic material with light brown complexion, rounded

face with full cheeks, tiny nose, small blue eyes with thick black eyeliner, short stroke brows, short brunette human hair, jointed curled arms and hands, straight toddler legs, wearing blue and white windowpane-print dress and panties, shoes and socks that appear original. Condition: generally excellent. Comments: Sasha Morgenthaler, circa 1950's, the model known as F bebe. Value Points: very rare studio Sasha doll to find, this example in wonderfully preserved condition. $4000/5000

70. Blonde-Haired Studio Toddler, F Bebe, by Sasha Morgenthaler
14" (35 cm.) Socket head and body of synthetic material with light tan complexion, rounded face with full cheeks, tiny nose, small brown eyes with thick black eyeliner, short stroke brows, long blonde human hair braids, jointed curled arms and hands, straight toddler legs, wearing red and white plaid dress dress and panties, shoes and socks that appear original. Condition: generally excellent. Marks: Sasha (tag inside dress and chemise). Comments: Sasha Morgenthaler, circa 1950's, the model known as F bebe. Value Points: among the rarest of the studio models, the perfectly preserved little toddler has endearing expression. $4000/5000

Cherries Jubilee

71. Italian Cloth Character Girl from Sports Series

14" (36 cm.). Felt swivel head with pressed and painted facial features, painted pale blue side-glancing eyes, dark eye shadow, painted lashes, accented nostrils, closed mouth with accented bottom lip, five piece felt body. Condition: generally excellent. Marks: (original Lenci paper label). Comments: Lenci, circa 1935. Value Points: rare model of blonde haired girl in rich green felt ski costume with appliqué argyle patterned vest, cuffs and hat trim, with leather boots, wooden skis, wooden ski poles with leather straps, white felt gloves, all preserved in crisp bright colors. $900/1500

72. Italian Cloth Rooster Girl by Lenci

15" (38 cm.) Felt swivel head with pressed and painted facial features, painted lashes, grey eye shadow, closed mouth, blonde mohair wig with silk ribbons enclosed braided coil, felt body with jointed arms and legs. Condition: generally excellent, some spotting on shawl and blouse. Comments: Lenci, circa 1935. Value Points: the little shy girl wears original folklore costume with green and black felt skirt and vest, green cotton plaid apron, wooden sole shoes with black felt straps, pantalets with green and black striping, and carrying a colorful felt rooster. $800/1100

73. Italian Cloth Girl by Lenci, Model 300/12

17" (43 cm.) Felt swivel head with pressed and painted facial features, brown side-glancing eyes, thickly fringed curly lashes, accented nostrils, closed mouth with accented bottom lip, blonde mohair wig in neat braided coil at back of head, five piece felt body. Condition: generally excellent. Marks: Lenci (feet, and three paper labels). Comments: Lenci, circa 1935, the model is 300/12 according to paper label. Value Points: superb costume is wonderfully preserved with vibrant colors, green shirt with orange and yellow trim, purple felt skit, blue felt apron with appliqué dots, felt bonnet with vibrant felt flowers, carrying wooden rake, crisp organdy undergarments, leather shoes. $1500/2000

74. Italian Black Cloth Character by Lenci

15" (38 cm.) Chubby toddler style doll of black felt, swivel head with rounded facial modeling and plump cheeks, white felt eyes with black shoe button centers, red nostrils, painted mouth, grey tightly fleeced hair, five piece body with plump belly, spread fingers, curled toes. Condition: generally excellent, few very minor repairs on belly. Comments: Lenci, circa 1935. Value Points: the very rare Lenci model is well-preserved, with original wooden alligator earrings, wooden beads with elephant dangles, grass skirt with felt ribbons. $2000/2500

75. Italian Black Cloth Character by Lenci
15" (38 cm.) Chubby toddler style doll of black felt, swivel head with rounded facial modeling and plump cheeks, white felt eyes with black shoe button centers, red nostrils, painted mouth, black curly hair, five piece body with plump belly, spread fingers, curled toes. Condition: generally excellent. Comments: Lenci, circa 1935. Value Points: very rare Lenci model with amusing detail including red felt belly-button, is well-preserved, with original wooden beads and earrings, grass skirt with felt ribbons. $2000/2500

76. Italian Glass-Eyed Googly Cloth Doll by Lenci
20" (51 cm.) Felt swivel head with pressed and painted facial features, wide-open glass googly eyes glancing to the right, "O" shaped mouth, V-shaped high brows, upturned nose, blonde mohair wig with side braids and tiny curled braid at the top of the head, five piece felt body with elongated slender legs, curved arms with spread fingers. Condition: generally excellent. Condition: Lenci, circa 1935. Value Points: fabulous model with most whimsical facial expression, wearing original red and white checkered top, green felt pants and shoes, with matching ribbons on braids, and carrying a mohair duckling with felt beak and feet, all preserved in crisp fresh colors. $2000/2500

Cherries Jubilee

77. French Bisque Bebe by Gaultier Freres
29" (74 cm.) Bisque socket head, large blue glass paperweight inset eyes, dark eye liner, painted dark lashes, widely brush-stroked brows, accented eye corners and nostrils, closed mouth with defined space between the shaded and outlined lips, plump cheek modeling, pierced ears, blonde mohair wig over cork pate, French composition and wooden fully-jointed body. Condition: generally excellent. Marks: 11 F.G. (in scroll). Comments: Gaultier Freres, circa 1888. Value Points: very expressive wide-eyed features on the well-modeled child doll, wearing lavish burgundy velvet dress with lace trim, undergarments, knit stockings, black leather shoes, fancy cap. $3500/4500

78. Very Rare French Bisque Portrait Doll by Van Rozen
15" (38 cm.) Bisque socket head portraying adult man with portrait like features, blue glass eyes set deeply into narrow eye sockets, tinted ochre eye shadow suggests lashes, arched brush-stroked brows, accented nostrils on strongly shaped nose, closed mouth with accent line between the lips, black curly mohair wig. French composition five-piece jointed body, wearing antique black woolen suit with blue patterned silk vest, shirt, tie, black beaver fur tall hat, shoes. Condition: generally excellent. Marks: Van Rozen France Depose (raised letters). Comments: Designed by artist Van Rozen, made in France, circa 1910. Value Points: very rare portrait model with most appealing expression from the French art doll movement, by named artist, and in fine smaller size. $7000/9000

79. Rare Early Mechanical Tricycle Rider Attributed to Vichy
7 1/2"l. (19 cm.) A bisque headed boy with black painted hair delicately stippled onto the forehead, painted facial features with bright blue eyes, metal hands

and feet, and wearing original costume of purple velvet jacket with gold edging, green silk trousers, is seated upon a three-wheeled metal tricycle with original red and green paint. When wound, the tricycle moves forward and in circles while the little boy appears to pedal. Condition: generally excellent. Comments: attributed to Vichy, circa 1865. Value Points: very rare little toy with wonderful presentation. $3000/4000

80. Pair, Chinese Wooden Door of Hope Bride and Groom
Each 12" (31 cm.) Each has carved wooden socket head with natural finish and tinted features, muslin body, wooden hands, and is wearing original costume, the Bride with carved black hair drawn away from face into coiled bun with decorative flowers, and wearing red silk wedding ensemble with elaborate decorated and beaded gown and head dress, slippers, pom-pom trims; and the Bridegroom with black short hair short black painted hair, wearing purple silk tunic with frog closures and embroidered medallion, pink silk tunic, purple silk pants, purple silk boots, black silk cap with tassel. Condition: generally excellent. Comments: from the Door of Hope mission of China, circa 1920. Value Points: well-preserved wedding couple in fine original costumes. $900/1400

81. Superb French Bisque Bebe Douillet for Jumeau
23" (58 cm.) Bisque socket head with unusual plump cheeks, small blue glass paperweight inset eyes with luminous depth, dark painted lashes and eyeliner, brush-stroked and multi-feathered brows, accented nostrils and eye corners, closed mouth with defined space between the shaded and outlined lips, pierced ears, dimpled chin, blonde mohair wig over cork pate, French composition and wooden fully jointed body. Condition: generally excellent. Marks: E. 9 D. (and artist check marks on head). Comments: Jumeau, circa 1890, the model's marking commemorated Jumeau's long-time loyal employee Douillet. Value Points: an exceptionally pretty French bebe with unusual expression, is perfectly preserved in virtually unplayed with condition, wearing original dress of burgundy silk and white patterned cashmere wool, undergarments, maroon knit stockings, fancy leather shoes with rosette trim signed L.D. and stored in its original French box. $6500/8500

Cherries Jubilee

82. French Bisque Automaton "The Cuisinier and Cat in the Kettle" by Roullet et Decamps

18" overall. Standing upon a velvet-covered wooden base is a bisque-headed doll with brown glass eyes, painted lashes and brows, closed mouth with accented lips, pierced ears, brunette mohair wig, carton torso and legs, wire upper arms, bisque forearms, alongside a tin stove with copper pot in which is hidden a white fur cat. When wound, music plays, and a series of amusing movements take place: the cuisinier turns his head, lifts and "drinks" from the wine bottle in his right hand, then lifts the lid of the cooking kettle and the cat pops out. Condition: generally excellent, mechanism and music function well. Marks: Tete Jumeau bte SGDG (head, along with artist checkmarks). Comments: Roullet et Decamps, the automaton was described in their 1890 era catalog and was offered with man or woman cook. Value Points: most amusing early automaton in superbly preserved condition including costume, accessories, and movement. $8000/10,000

83. Extremely Rare and Beautiful French Bisque Bebe Triste, Size 16, by Jumeau

33" (84 cm.) Pressed bisque socket head, large blue glass paperweight inset eyes of great depth, dark eyeliner, painted lashes, mauve blushed eye shadow, brush-stroked and multi-feathered brows, accented eye corners, shaded nostrils, closed mouth with defined space between the pale outlined lips with accent touches, dimpled blushed chin, separately modeled pierced ears with blushing detail, brunette mohair wig over cork pate. French composition and wooden fully jointed body with very plump limbs. Condition: generally excellent. Marks: 16 (head) Jumeau Medaille d'Or Paris (body). Comments: Emile Jumeau, circa 1884, the model known as Bebe Triste in reference to its wistful sad expression. Value Points: extremely rare size of the desirable model, few models in this size are known to exist, with deeply sculpted facial features, finest bisque with luminous patina, original body with original finish, and wearing superb original ivory silk party costume with rose silk pom-poms and sash, undergarments, shoes. $22,000/28,000

84. All-Original French Musical Marotte

13" (33 cm.) A bisque-headed doll with blue glass eyes and blonde mohair ringlet curls is attached to carved wooden upper torso, hollow ball lower torso with music box inside, and wooden hands, the entire posed upon a polished Maplewood stick handle. The doll is dressed in original ivory and rose silk harlequin style costume with silver fringe and bells, and with matching cap. When twirled around, the costume flaps merrily wave, and music is heard. Comments: for the French market, circa 1890. Value Points: superbly preserved marotte with unusually fine quality of music box. $900/1300

85. German Bisque Jester with Blinking Eyes by Zinner and Sohne

13" (33 cm.) Bisque socket head, blue glass eyes, exaggerated painting of facial features, long pointy nose, mouth with hinged jaw, painted teeth, blonde mohair wig, bellows torso under muslin costume, wooden hands and feet. When bellows squeezed in torso, the jester blinks his eyes, mouth opens and closes and hands clap the cymbals that he holds. Condition: generally excellent. Comments: attributed to Zinner and Sohne, circa 1890. Value Points: rare and amusing toy with three movements, wearing original factory costume. $1200/1800

Cherries Jubilee

84A. French Bisque Automaton "Little Girl with Polichinelle and Rattle" by Roullet et Decamps

20" (52 cm.) A bisque-headed doll with blue glass eyes, mohair lashes, open mouth, blonde mohair wig, carton torso, composition legs, wire upper arms, bisque forearms, wearing aqua and ivory silk costume and Polichinelle cap, is seated upon a maple wood bench, and holds a toy in each hand. When wound a series of movements occur: the doll turns her head side to side, nods her head, blinks her eyes, kicks her right foot to the side in a happy gesture, and alternately plays with the richly carved bone rattle she holds in her right hand and the bisque-headed Polichinelle doll she holds in her left hand; music plays all the while. Condition: generally excellent. Marks: SH (head). Comments: Roullet et Decamps, circa 1900. Value Points: wonderful automaton with five well-functioning movements, most appealing activities with matching-costumed Polichinelle, lovely music. $6500/9500

85A. Wonderful French Bisque "Gigoteur" by Steiner with Au Nain Bleu Costume

23" (58 cm.) Solid domed bisque head with flat-cut neck socket, rounded facial modeling, large blue glass paperweight inset eyes, dark eye liner, painted lashes, brush-stroked and feathered brows, rose blushed eye shadow, accented nostrils and eye corners, open mouth, outlined and shaded lips, two rows of tiny teeth, pierced ears, blonde mohair wig with original paper label "3", carton torso with mechanical clockwork interior, composition arms and lower legs. When keywound, the doll turns head from side to side, waves arms and legs and cries "mama". Condition: generally excellent. Comments: Jules Steiner, circa 1885, the unusually large size of his bebe functions well, wears lavish original costume with original label from Paris toy store Au Nain Bleu, including extravagant bonnet, leather shoes signed with figure of doll. $3000/4000

86. French All-Bisque Mignonette with Jointed Elbows and Bare Feet

5 1/2" (14 cm.) Bisque swivel head with cut pate, blue glass enamel inset eyes, tinted eye lids, single stroke brows, accented eye corners, closed mouth with center accent line, peg-jointed bisque arms and legs, ball-jointed elbows, bare feet. Condition: generally excellent. Marks: Bte. Comments: the jointed elbow model was deposed by Sustrac in 1877. Value Points: desirable and very rare mignonette model has jointed elbows, original wig and costume. $4000/5500

87. French Bisque Mechanical Tricyclist by Vichy

11"l. (28 cm.) Seated upon a cast metal tricycle with large spoked wheels and original red and black stenciled paint is a bisque-headed man with brown sculpted hair, goatee and moustache, with painted blue eyes, brows, and closed mouth, and wearing original silk costume and cap. When wound, the tricycle moves forward and in circles, and the rider appears to turn the pedals. Condition: generally excellent, mechanism functions well. Comments: Vichy, circa 1865. Value Points: rare early mechanical toy with original costume, painting, well-functioning. $3500/4500

88. French Bisque Bebe E.J, Size 8, by Emile Jumeau

18" (46 cm.) Pressed bisque socket head, blue glass paperweight inset eyes, dark eyeliner, painted lashes, mauve blushed eye shadow, accented eye corners, shaded nostrils, closed mouth, defined space between the shaded and outlined lips, separately modeled pierced ears, blonde mohair wig over cork pate, French composition and wooden fully-jointed body with straight wrists. Condition: generally excellent. Marks: Depose E. 8 J. (head) Jumeau Medaille d'Or Paris (body). Comments: Emile Jumeau, circa 1884. Value Points: superb example of the beautiful EJ model with finest quality of bisque, original wig, pate, body, body finish, antique dress, bonnet, undergarments, leather boots, socks. $5500/7500

Cherries Jubilee

89A. Outstanding Early French Sewing Necessaire
11" x 8". A wooden framed domed box with serpentine shape is richly covered in purple velvet with metallic and bead thread, and bronze mountings, and opens to a beautifully fitted interior with various bone sewing implements, gold thimble, brass sampler stencils, wooden embroidery hoop, little boxes with lithographed covers containing pins, buttons and such; a hidden compartment contains an assortment of sewing accessories collected by the original user including an intriguing maple wood pin cushion from the same era with a design of the United States Capitol Building in Washington. Excellent condition. French, circa 1880. $800/1200

90. Five Bisque Theatre Dolls and Miniature Musical Chaise a Porteur
5" dolls. Each of five dolls has bisque shoulder heads, blonde sculpted hair, painted facial features, muslin body, bisque lower limbs, and each is wearing

89. Early Period French Porcelain Poupee by Leontine Rohmer with Trunk and Costumes
16" (41 cm.) Thick paste porcelain swivel head with flat-cut neck socket that fits into complementary shoulder plate, painted facial features, blue upper glancing eyes with thick upper eyeliner and fringed lashes, feathered brows, accented nostrils, closed mouth with pert smile, blonde mohair wig over cork pate, kid body with gusset-jointed upper legs, ball-jointed knees with enclosed within kid lower legs, kid-over-wood upper arms, porcelain arms from above the elbows, separately sculpted fingers with painted nails. Condition: generally excellent. Marks: Mme Rohmer Brevete SGDG (body stamp), circa 1860, the doll evidences two early Rohmer patents, viz. head attachment through unique stringing at the pate, and system for sitting by means of two grommet holes in torso for string attachment. Value Points: exquisite early Rohmer poupee with wonderful face, swivel neck, original signed body, wearing fine original costume, and owning her original trunk with two additional dresses, capes, hat in hat box, fan in original box, Loto game, leather purse, and various undergarments. $9000/12,000

its original factory made theatre costume to represent Marquis, Marquise, another lady, and two jesters. Along with French miniature chaise a porteur with enameled designs of young cherubs, with maroon velvet trim and beveled glass windows, with hidden music box that winds from beneath. Condition: generally excellent. Comments: made for the French market by Charles Keller who registered a design for the dolls in 1877. Value Points: wonderful original costumes on the theatre dolls, perfectly sized for display with the chaise a porteur having rare musical device. $900/1300

904. French Bisque Poupee in Superb Original Costume
15" (38 cm.) Bisque swivel head on kid-edged bisque shoulder plate, cobalt blue glass enamel inset eyes, dark eyeliner encircles the eyecut, painted lashes and brows, accented nostrils, closed mouth with accented lips, ears pierced into head, blonde mohair wig over cork pate, kid fashion body with shapely waist, gusset-jointing at hips and knees. Condition: generally excellent. Comments: circa 1867. Value Points: the beautiful cobalt-blue eyed poupee with lovely bisque is wearing her original undergarments, leather slippers, exquisite mauve silk fashion gown with Alencon lace and silk ribbons, and long train, pearl necklace, and dainty bonnet with floral trim. $3500/4500

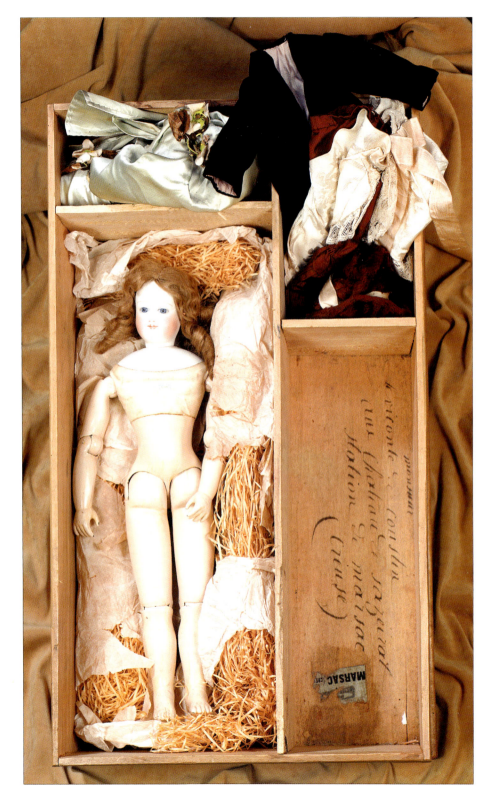

91. Very Rare French Bisque Poupee by Pierre Clement with Original Box and Provenance
17" (45 cm.) Bisque swivel head on kid-edged bisque shoulder plate, blue glass enamel inset eyes, painted lashes, feathered brows, accented nostrils, closed mouth, accented lips, brunette human hair over cork pate, blown kid body with dowel-jointing at shoulders, elbows, hips and knees. Condition: generally excellent. Marks: Vtr. Clement. Solidite. Garante (green stamp on torso). Comments: Victor Pierre Clement who registered his unique doll body in 1866, just prior to the 1867 Universal Exposition in Paris, claiming these bodies were the "most beautiful, lightest and most rugged made to date". Value Points: in superb original condition, the rare poupee is preserved in its original box along with several original gowns; the box bearing the address "Monsieur le viconte de coustin aux Chateau de Sazeirat, Station de Marsac (Creuse)". $10,000/15,000

92. French Bisque Poupee with Portrait-like Face, attributed to Dehors
20" (51 cm.) Bisque swivel head with distinctive oval shape, on kid-edged bisque shoulder plate, head and neck attachment based on the Dehors system allowing the head to tilt forward and side to side as well as pivot, cobalt blue glass enamel eyes, dark eyeliner, painted lashes, feathered brows, accented nostrils and eye corners, closed mouth with accented lips, ears pierced into head, blonde mohair wig over cork pate, kid fashion body with gusset hips and knees, kid over wooden upper arms, bisque arms to above the dimpled elbows, lovely gown of antique fabrics, undergarments, leather boots. Condition: generally excellent, right thumb broken, tiny flake at back shoulder plate neck. Comments: attributed to Dehors, who deposed the life-like head/shoulder attachment in 1866 in time for exhibition of his poupees at the 1867 Universal Exposition in Paris. Value Points: very beautiful regal portrait lady with rare depose feature and lovely bisque, fine larger size. $4000/4500

92A. Two Gilded Doll Chairs in the Italian Renaissance Style
15" (38 cm.) The wood framed chairs with richly carved columns and medallions are finished in gold leaf, and have delicate silk upholstery, comprising larger arm chair with padded arm rests, and smaller side chair. With remnants of original paper labels on base of each. Probably late 19th century. $500/700

Cherries Jubilee

Cherries Jubilee

93. Superb Large French Bisque Bebe Steiner, Figure C
33" (84 cm.) Bisque socket head with rounded facial modeling, brown glass paperweight inset eyes, thick dark eyeliner, painted delicate lashes, rose blushed eye shadow, brush-stroked brows, accented eye corners, shaded nostrils, closed mouth with defined space between the shaded lips, pierced ears, blonde mohair wig over Steiner pate. Steiner composition fully jointed body. Condition: generally excellent. Marks: Figure C. No 7 (incised on head) J. Steiner Bte SGDG Paris (script on head) Le Petit Parisien Bebe Steiner (body). 7 (pate). Comments: Jules Steiner, circa 1884. Value Points: superb large

bebe with finest quality of bisque and modeling, gorgeous eyes, original body, body finish with distinctive Steiner fingernail outlines, pate, and bronze silk faille dress with velvet trim bearing original label from Au Bon Marche store in Paris, undergarments, shoes. $8000/11,000

93A. French Bisque Automaton "Little Girl with Drum" by Roullet et Decamps
19" (48 cm.) overall. Standing upon a velvet covered wooden base is a bisque-head girl with brown glass paperweight inset eyes and closed mouth, blonde mohair wig, carton torso and legs, wire upper arms, bisque forearms, rose silk and lace costume and elaborate bonnet. In front of the girl is a wooden framed drum with elaborate braid perched upon a metal base, and when wound, the girl turns her head back and forth and alternately taps the drum and then the cymbal, in time to the music which plays in the background. Marks: Depose Tete Jumeau 1 (doll). Comments: Roullet et Decamps, circa 1890. Value Points: rare and amusing automaton featuring doll with most beautiful face, well-functioning movements and music. $7500/9500

94. Extremely Rare Early French Paper Mache Soldier
12" (30 cm.) Of very lightweight hollow paper mache, the articulated doll portrays an early 19th century French soldier, having articulated head, arms and legs, with painted and sculpted hair and facial features, smiling expression, separately modeled hat with painted French emblem attached to head with metal pin, sculpted and painted military costume including details such as painted buttons, high leggings, and cuffs. Condition: generally excellent, painted finish is all original albeit with pleasing faded patina. Comments: French, circa 1840. Value Points: few street bazaar toys of this period still exist, this remarkable example in fine condition and most appealing. $2000/2500

94A. An All Original French Bisque Poupee by Gaultier with Costume
15" (38 cm.) Bisque swivel head on kid-edged bisque shoulder plate, brown glass enamel inset eyes, painted lashes, brush-stroked and feathered brows, accented nostrils and eye corners, closed mouth, accented lips, pierced ears, blonde mohair wig over cork pate, kid gusset-jointed body with stitched and separated fingers. Condition: generally excellent. Marks: 2 (head). Comments: Gaultier, circa 1880. Value Points: in

fine unplayed with condition, wearing original muslin chemise, the doll also owns an exquisite brown silk gown with matching bonnet, fur stole, undergarments, leather ankle boots with tiny heels signed "2" and "P" (in script). $2800/3500

95. All-Original French Bisque Poupee by Gaultier
15" (38 cm.) Bisque swivel head on kid-edged bisque shoulder plate, brown glass enamel inset eyes, painted lashes, feathered brows, accented eye corners and nostrils, closed mouth with accented lips, pierced ears, blonde mohair wig over cork pate, French kid gusset-jointed body, stitched and separated fingers. Condition: generally excellent. Marks: 2 (head). Comments: Gaultier, circa 1880. Value Points: very beautiful expression with large eyes, unplayed with condition, with original ribbon-tied wig, earrings, and muslin chemise. $2500/3000

Cherries Jubilee

96. Fine Early German Paper Mache Doll with Elaborate Coiffure
23" (58 cm.) Paper mache shoulder head with oval-shaped face, very elongated strong throat and modeled bosom, sculpted hair in elaborate arrangement with center part, tight curls at each side of face, and coiled braid atop the head, exposed ears, painted facial features, downward-glancing shaded turquoise eyes, black upper eyeliner, feathered brows, closed mouth with accented pale lips, early muslin stitch-jointed body, leather arms with separated fingers, nicely costumed in appropriately styled gown, undergarments, antique slippers. Condition: split across the back shoulder plate (under costume), otherwise the finish is original and virtually flawless with a fine patina. Comments: Germany, circa 1840. Value Points: very rare early model with elaborate coiffure, modeled bosom, large size. $1700/2500

97. Set of Wooden Puzzle Blocks in Original Box
15" x 11" (38 x 28 cm assembled). A wooden box contains a large set of wooden six-sided puzzles with engravings of early Victorian scenes enabling six different puzzles to be created. Sheets with engravings of five of the puzzles are included, with varnished detail (rehaussee) to enhance the image. All of the images feature children, and two include dolls. Printed by F. Silber, Berlin. Circa 1850. $500/800

98. "Le Trousseau de La Poupee" Paper Doll in Original Box
10 1/2" (27 cm.) doll. A double sided paper doll with chemise and curved right arm with six exquisite double-sided gowns, seven double-sided collars or shoulder wraps, one long pair of gloves, and ten double-sided bonnets with elaborate arrangements of hair. Condition: generally excellent. Comments: French, circa 1850. Value Points: extremely rare early paper doll made notable for its bonnets with variations of coiffure, and its original box whose lid depicts a little girl playing with the paper doll. $1500/2200

99. Early Wooden Doll with Cage Skirt
23" (59 cm.) One piece carved wooden head to torso with oval-shaped face, elongated throat, and shapely torso with tiny waist, painted facial features with sculpted definition of eye sockets, aquiline nose, full lips, delicate hemp wig, fabric covered wire armature arms with elegantly carved wooden hands, cage-shaped base under skirt, antique gown of silks and fine muslin with embroidery and metallic threads. Condition: good, some restoration under the chin. Comments: Early 19th century, remnants of German language papers under the cage. Value Points: appealing enigmatic expression of the early example of fashion doll, quite rare to find. $2000/3000

100. French Mahogany and Maple Cabinet Maker's Secretaire of the 1830 Epoch
23" (59 cm.) The early desk with marble top is made of fine mahogany with maple wood interiors and maple wood striped veneers outlining the leather writing surface, with three drawers, ogee-shaped crest, four miniature drawers and niche, with lock and key. French, circa 1830, the quality of construction and woods indicates the desk was made as a maitrise model by skilled cabinet maker. Included are five miniature children's books: Le Petit Conteur with engravings (c. 1850), Les Psaumes de David (1837), Souvenirs d'un Petit Vogageur (c. 1850), and two others. $1200/1800

101. Early French Cherry Wood Doll Chair
12" (30 cm.) Of fine polished cherry wood, the chairs features an intricately carved back of unusual design, carved front legs and stretcher, and tightly woven cane seat. Excellent condition. French, circa 1850. $500/700

102. Two Early 19th Century Cast Wax Miniature Arrangements in Domes
5" (13 cm) h. smaller. Each arrangement features a cast wax figure of a child, one with sunbonnet and little lamb in garden setting, the other a girl with bucket standing beside the well under a bower of gilded flowers, each enclosed within blown glass dome, one dome being a very unique round shape, on original bases. Early 19th century. Excellent condition, and extremely rare to find. $800/1000

Cherries Jubilee

103. Fine Early German Porcelain Doll
17" (45 cm.) Porcelain shoulder head of lady with slender face, elongated throat, deeply sloping shoulders, black sculpted hair drawn to below ears and waved backward, exposing the ears into coiled braided bun at back of head, painted blue eyes, red and black eyeliner, single stroke brows, accented nostrils and eye corners, closed mouth, accented lips, muslin stitch-jointed body, porcelain limbs, antique gown and undergarments, leather shoes. Condition: possible restoration to shoulder plate, virtually undefinable. Comments: Germany, circa 1850. Value Points: very beautiful early porcelain doll with wonderful face, elaborate coiffure, quite rare to find. $800/1200

104. Early Fireplace and Mirrored Mantle
23" (58 cm.) overall. Wooden framed fireplace in original ebony finish with white interiors, black diamond tiled floor, opening tin plate fire door, surmounted by a wooden mantle with faux-cabinet doors and a rich gilt ormolu mirror, along with wooden bellows and brass fire tool. A superb and very rare miniature furnishing, suitable sized for display with 12"-17" dolls, the fireplace is hand-lettered on the reverse "Etrennes 1880" indicating its origin as a Christmas season gift in 1880. $1200/1800

105. French Bisque Poupee Attributed to Leon Casimir Bru
17" (45 cm.) Pale bisque swivel head on kid-edged bisque shoulder plate, blue glass enamel inset eyes, dark eyeliner, painted lashes, feathered brows, accented nostrils, closed mouth, accented lips with hint of smile, ears pierced into head, blonde mohair wig over cork pate, kid fashion body with shapely

torso, kid over wooden upper arms, bisque arms to above the elbows, with separately sculpted fingers, nicely costumed in gown of vintage mauve silk, undergarments, leather slippers. Condition: generally excellent, left baby finger broken. Marks: F (head and shoulder plate). Comments: from the letter series of Leon Casimir Bru, circa 1865. Value Points: very compelling dreamy expression is wonderfully achieved on the early signed poupee with especially sturdy body, choice bisque. $3000/3500

106. An All-Original German Bisque Doll with Unusual Costume
10" (25 cm.) Bisque shoulder head with pale complexion, painted facial features, cobalt blue eyes, red and black upper eyeliner, single stroke brows, accented nostrils, closed mouth, brunette wig coiffed into tiniest braids with interwoven blue ribbons, muslin body, carved wooden hands and legs with painted black ankle boots. Condition: generally excellent. Comments: Germany, circa 1870. Value Points: in fine unplayed with condition, the doll wears original red knit dress and jacket trimmed with cream and black borders, with fancy tasseled cap, in fresh vibrant condition and colors. $900/1300

107. French Miniature Food in Grocery Box
3 1/2"l. (9 cm.) A woven basket with wooden frame hinges open to reveal miniature faux-food, and original paper label "Le Delicieux" from the Maison Grenier in Pont L'Eveque in Calvados, France. Circa 1890. $300/400

108. Miniature French Fortune-Telling Doll
6" (15 cm.) Bisque shoulder head with short blonde sculpted curly hair, painted features, muslin torso, bisque lower limbs, wearing original black velvet and red silk gown with lace trim. Condition: generally excellent. Comments: for the French market, circa 1880. Value Points: the doll has a hidden "skirt" of folded paper fortunes; when unfolded each leaf has contains a message for the reader; this is an unusually rare small size of the classic 19th century toy. $800/1100

109. German Bisque Fashion Lady with Earrings and Necklace
14" (35 cm.) Bisque shoulder head with blonde sculpted hair waved away from face and captured by gild-edged black hair band, sculpted earrings and black ribbon necklace with white cross dangle, painted facial features, outlined blue eyes with painted lashes, feathered brows, accented nostrils, closed mouth with center accent line, old muslin body with wooden hands and lower legs, painted orange ankle boots, wearing antique white fitted gown and undergarments. Condition: generally excellent. Comments: Germany, circa 1870. Value Points: rarity factors include fancy coiffure, earrings, necklace, painted lashes. $800/1200

Cherries Jubilee

Cherries Jubilee

110. Pair, German Squeek Toys
3" diameter larger. Each is of paper mache with sculpted and painted facial features and hair. each with faces on either side of a ball-shaped head and leather bellows in between. creating a squeeking cry when squeezed. include doll head with sculpted brown hair. and black doll head with smiling face on one side. and crying face on the other. Circa 1880. a very rare pair of early doll-head squeek toys in fine original finish. well-functioning. $700/1000

111. French Paper Mache Poupee in Brittany Costume
18" (46 cm.) Solid domed paper mache shoulder head with painted black pate. black enamel glass inset eyes, painted lashes. feathered brows. accented nostrils. open mouth. accented lips. two rows of tiny teeth. pink kid fashion body with shapely torso and limbs. stitched and separated fingers. Condition: generally excellent. Comments: French. circa 1855. Value Points: the early fashion doll model has fine original finish and sturdy body. and is wearing her original richly embroidered costume of Brittany along with elaborate lace coiffe. undergarments. and shoes. $1200/1500

112. Early German Tinplate and Enamel Toy Stove
19"h. (49 cm.) The wooden framed toy stove has tinplate sides and burners and ash drawer. decorative blue and white enamel stove front with embossed tin border. wooden back with paper lithographed tile design. shelf. with three enameled pots or spoon and tin utensil. Very good condition. some wear to black paint of tinplate. A rare style of early toy stove. Circa 1880. $800/1000

113. German Paper Mache Child in Original Folklore Costume
14" (36 cm.) Paper mache shoulder head with large blue glass inset eyes with spiral threading. painted lashes. feathered brows. closed mouth with accented lips. brunette mohair wig. muslin body. composition lower limbs. Condition: generally excellent. Comments: Germany. circa 1885. Value Points: especially pretty child with original body. wearing wonderful elaborate original folklore costume with superb coiffe and cobbler-made wooden soled leather boots. $900/1400

114. French Wooden and Bone Miniature Spinning Wheel
14" (36 cm.) Elaborately carved wooden spinning wheel with dark finish and inlay heart design. wooden decorative dangles. and carved bone finials and trim. actually works when foot pedal pressed. labeled "Strasbourg" on pedal. Excellent condition of the superbly detailed miniature. French. circa 1880. $1200/1800

115. French Paper Mache Poupee in Nun's Habit with Bisque Baby
21" (54 cm.) Solid domed paper mache shoulder head with oval shaped face and elongated throat. black enamel inset eyes, black painted pate. feathered lashes and brows. aquiline-shaped nose. closed mouth with pale accented lips. old muslin stitch-jointed body. Condition: generally excellent. Comments: French. circa 1850. Value Points: with most compelling serene expression. the doll wears original detailed nun's habit including miniature cross and rosary. and is carrying miniature bisque doll with sculpted brown hair and painted facial features (probably early Gaultier) wearing hand-made detailed woolen baby ensemble. $2200/2800

Cherries Jubilee

116. All-Original German Composition Character by Marian Kaulitz
13" (33 cm.) Composition socket head, painted facial features, small brown eyes with white eye dots, upper eyeliner, lightly feathered brows, accented nostrils, closed mouth with very full rosy lips, blushed cheeks, brunette mohair wig, composition and wooden ball-jointed body. Condition: generally excellent. Comments: from the art character series dolls of Marian Kaulitz, circa 1908.

considered the inspiration for the entire German art doll series of the next five years. Value Points: superb pristine condition of the all-original doll, fine lustrous patina of complexion, soft mohair curls, original body finish, original folklore costume and black leather shoes. $2000/3000

117. Rare German Multi-Head Character Series by Kestner in Unusual Small Size
11" (28 cm.) Contained within its original box is a bisque doll along with three alternate bisque heads to be used interchangeably with the body: the doll has brown glass sleep eyes, open mouth, blonde mohair wig over plaster pate, composition and wooden ball-jointed body, original muslin chemise, shoes and socks, and is marked 174; the alternate heads each have painted eyes and mohair wigs, as follows: model 178 with solemn expression and brown eyes; 185 with smiling expression and brown eyes, 184 with pouty expression and blue eyes.

Condition: generally excellent. Marks: (see above). Comments: Kestner, circa 1911, the dolls are presented in original box labeled "Kestner character doll" in English, and original price of $3.69, indicating its production for the American market. Value Points: pristine unplayed with condition of the set, in rare smaller size. $7000/10,000

118. German Paper Mache Bunny Clown Candy Container
6" (15 cm.) Paper mache one-eared bunny with tiny brown glass eyes and modeled cap has removable head for candy storage in his torso; with modeled yellow clown costume with green and red buttons, ruffled collar, and orange shoes. Excellent condition. Germany, circa 1910. $500/700

119. German Pull-Toy Cow
8 1/2" (22 cm.) Paper mache cow with flocked finish to simulate hide has brown glass eyes, udder, wooden hooves with tinplate wheels, and is decorated with leatherette straps trimmed with silver medallions, red felt mantel with silver band and pull chain. Very fine original condition. Germany, circa 1900. $500/700

120. German All-Bisque Googly
4" (10 cm.) One piece bisque head and torso, painted facial features, blue side-glancing eyes, button-shaped nose, closed mouth, brunette mohair wig, loop-jointed bisque arms and legs with painted blue stockings and black shoes. Condition: generally excellent, string loop repaired on right leg. Comments: Germany, circa 1920. Value Points: amusing little imp in tiny size, original wig. $300/400

121. German All-Bisque Googly
5" (13 cm.) One piece bisque head and torso, painted facial features, large blue side-glancing eyes with white eye dots, painted lashes and brows, button-shaped nose, closed mouth, loop-jointed bisque arms and legs. Condition: generally excellent, legs are not original. Comments: Germany, circa 1920. Value Points: especially fine detail of googly eyes. $300/400

122. 19th Century Pull-Toy Cow on Wheels with "Moo" Bellows
25" (64 cm.) A firm-sided paper mache cow covered in brown and cream hide has realistic sculpting, glass inset eyes, carved nostrils and mouth, horns, udder, and wooden hooves with cast iron wheels beneath. There is a hidden funnel so the cow can be actually "milked" and the elaborate leather harness with cow bell hides a neck joint that, when gently pushed, causes the cow to "moo". Excellent condition of the rare and well-preserved toy in fine large size. $1500/2000

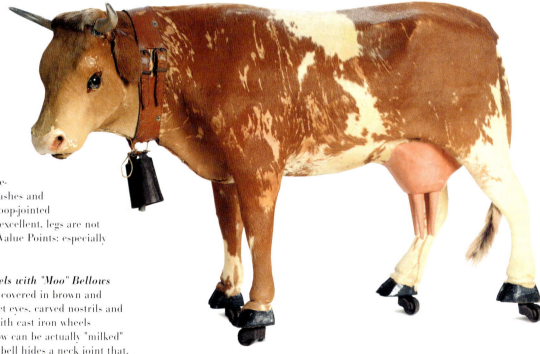

Cherries Jubilee

123. German Bisque Pouty, "Gretchen" by Kammer and Reinhardt
18" (46 cm.) Bisque socket head, deeply sculpted and painted facial features, shaded blue eyes with white eye dots, black and incised upper eyeliner, short tapered brows, accented nostrils, closed mouth with accented lips, blonde mohair wig, composition and wooden ball-jointed body, antique costume, undergarments, and boots. Condition: generally excellent. Marks: K*R 114 46. Comments: Kammer and Reinhardt, "Gretchen" from the art character series, circa 1909. Value Points: especially fine example of the model with superb sculpting, fine lustrous patina of bisque, original wig, body and body finish. $4500/6500

124. Large German Bisque Pouty, "Hans" by Kammer and Reinhardt
23" (57 cm.) Bisque socket head, painted facial features, shaded blue eyes with decorative glaze, thick black upper eyeliner, incised eyeliner, tapered one stroke brows, accented nostrils, closed mouth, shaded lips, brunette fleeced hair, composition and wooden ball-jointed body, antique boy's costume including blue velvet coat, britches, argyle socks, leather shoes and cap. Condition: generally excellent, few typical wig pulls. Marks: K*R 114 57. Comments: Kammer and Reinhardt, circa 1909. Value Points: wonderful large size allowing full expression of the pouty features, very full lips and impressed fret lines, choice bisque, original body and body finish, wonderful costume. $6500/8500

125. Rare German Bisque Portrait by Bawo and Dotter
16" (41 cm.) Bisque shoulderhead with slender heart-shaped face, brown glass inset eyes, painted lashes, feathered brows, accented nostrils and eye corners, closed mouth with center accent line, brunette mohair wig, muslin body with stitch-jointed limbs, sewn on blue leather shoes, bisque forearms, antique cotton gown and apron, straw bonnet, undergarments. Condition: generally excellent. Marks: 215 1 B&D Ltd Germany. Comments: Bawo and Dotter, circa 1910, a very rare series of character bisque dolls was produced by this firm and are considered some of the finest of the entire art character movement. Value Points: most beautiful facial expression with unusual facial shape, wistful look, choice bisque and painting. $4500/6500

Cherries Jubilee

126. Miniature Toy Sewing Machine
6"l. (15 cm.) Tin and iron toy sewing machine with painted floral decorations and painted self-case into which the machine can be lowered to form a closed box, actually functions by turning the handle. Germany, circa 1890. $200/300

127. German Bisque Character, 150, by Simon and Halbig
16" (41 cm.) Bisque socket head with slender facial modeling of older child, painted facial features, deeply set eyes with shaded blue coloring and upward glance, black upper eyeliner, one stroke tapered brows, closed mouth with richly shaded lips, blonde mohair braids, composition and wooden ball-jointed body, nicely costumed. Condition: generally excellent, chip on inside head rim. Marks: 150 S&H 0 1/2. Comments: Simon and Halbig, circa 1910, from their art character series. Value Points: especially fine sculpting details with deeply impressed facial features of solemn-faced young lady, choice bisque and painting, original body and body finish. $7000/9000

Cherries Jubilee

128. American Wooden Character by Schoenhut
16" (41 cm.) Carved/pressed wooden socket head, painted facial features, brown eyes with prominent black pupils, white eyedots, fringed lashes, closed mouth with pouty expression, original brunette mohair tacked on wig, wooden spring-jointed body, antique calico dress, undergarments, black stockings, original Schoenhut shoes. Condition: generally excellent. Marks: Schoenhut Doll. Pat. Jan.17 '11. USA and Foreign Countries. Comments: Schoenhut, circa 1915. Value Points: rare model with beautifully preserved original finish, wistful expression, original wig, and rare style original shoes. $1100/1300

129. American Wooden "Black Dude" and Buffalo by Schoenhut
7 1/2" (19 cm.) excluding hat. Man with dark brown complexion, painted facial features, smiling expression with painted teeth, hair, all wooden body, with original purple felt coat, yellow vest, checkered pants, top hat, marketed by Schoenhut as "Black Dude" and sometimes appearing as "African Chief, Style II"; along with glass-eyed buffalo with cloth ruff and open mouth. Excellent condition. Circa 1915. $1100/1400

130. American Wooden "Koko" and Bisque Head Clown by Schoenhut
8" and 10". The larger clown, Koko, has white clown painted complexion with "O" shaped eyes and diamond point brows, red nose and wide red mouth, and is wearing original black cotton clown suit and cap with white felt pom-poms and white edging, based upon the cartoon character created by the Fleischer brothers in 1915 in a series of early animation strips from their "Out of the Inkwell" studios; Koko and the cartoon strip were popular from 1915 until 1927 although largely forgotten today. Along with unusual bisque-headed clown with painted decorations and glass eyes, on classic Schoenhut body with original clown costume. Both excellent condition. Koko is one of the rarest of the Schoenhut figures. Circa 1918. $2500/3500

131. American Wooden Circus by Schoenhut
8" clown. The standard size circus includes six animals (polar bear with glass eyes and open mouth; single-hump camel with glass eyes and closed mouth; brown bear with glass eyes and open mouth; pig with painted eyes and open mouth; goose with painted eyes; and black-faced monkey with original costume) and three persons (clown with pink and white costume; Hobo with brown jacket; and first style Chinese acrobat with two-part head, blue jacket). Along with metal animal cage with platform, three chairs and red performing platform. All very good to excellent condition, monkey and pig tail replaced, one goose foot missing, the other replaced, and hat on clown replaced. Circa 1912. $1500/2000

Cherries Jubilee

132. American Wooden Circus by Schoenhut
8" clown. The standard size circus includes six animals (white-faced monkey with original costume; glass-eyed zebra with closed mouth; glass-eyed tiger with dowel-jointed neck and open mouth; glass-eyed elephant; glass-eyed donkey with open mouth; and glass-eyed poodle with cloth mane and open mouth) four people (Ringmaster with two-part head and original costume; Hobo with two part head and original costume; Chinaman, and Clown with two part head; and metal animal cage, one chair, two ladders, ball, barrel and stool. Good to excellent condition, ears replaced on donkey, costume not original Chinaman and his ears and part of one foot are missing, original finish on clown worn. Schoenhut, circa 1912. $1200/1600

133. Schoenhut Spark Plug and Barney Google
7 1/2" including hat. All wooden Barney Google with smaller head, carved definition of eyes and nose, attached wooden tall hat, with original costume comprising black felt jacket, white shirt, black and white checkered pants; along with Spark Plug, and original paper label "Copyright 1922 by King Features Syn., Pat Applied for". Excellent condition, blanket replaced. Schoenhut, circa 1922. $500/700

134. Schoenhut Max and Moritz with Pig and Wheelbarrow
8" dolls. Max with two part head and black sculpted hair and painted facial features, wearing original blue jacket, print shirt, black and white checkered pants; and Moritz with one part head, brown painted hair, wearing green felt jacket, belt, homespun pants. Along with glass-eyed pin with open mouth, and red wooden wheelbarrow. Moritz appears restored with paint worn on hands. Max has paint worn on hands; originality of wheelbarrow uncertain. Schoenhut, circa 1912. $800/1100

135. Schoenhut Black Clown and Glass-eyed Lion
8" clown. Black-complexioned clown with painted facial features, wide beaming smile with teeth, painted flocked hair, all wooden body with slits in hands and feet for positioning, original clown costume; along with glass-eyed lion with carved mane, and closed mouth. Excellent condition, some spotting on clown costume. Schoenhut, circa 1912. $700/900

Cherries Jubilee

136. German Bisque Toddler, 116A, by Kammer and Reinhardt 21" (53 cm.) Bisque socket head, brown glass sleep eyes, dark eyeliner, painted lashes, short feathered brows, accented nostrils and eye corners, closed mouth with modeled space between the smiling lips, two beaded teeth, brunette human hair in side braids, composition and wooden ball-jointed toddler body, antique costume. Condition: generally excellent. Marks: K*R Simon & Halbig 116/A. Comments: Kammer and Reinhardt, circa 1915. Value Points: wonderful definition of character features, choicest bisque and painting, great body with chubby tummy, original body finish. $1500/1800

137. Schoenhut Animal Parade Wagon with Gorilla

wagon 17", overall 28". A wooden framed wagon with sculpted gesso decorations on the crest and base depicting woman's head and the words "Humpty Dumpty Circus" has gilded columns, wire cage rods, wooden wheels with carved detail, opening door at the back, driver's seat with driver having light brown painted hair, moustache and sideburns, and being pulled by two dappled wooden horses on wooden platform. Inside the cage is the Schoenhut wooden gorilla with two-part head and leather ears. Condition: gorilla in excellent condition, platform, tack, and driver's coat and hat replaced. Comments: Schoenhut, circa 1912. Value Points: one of the four parade wagons made by Schoenhut, and very rare to find; the gorilla is exceptionally rare particularly this first period model in fine condition. $7000/9000

138. Five Schoenhut Circus Performers with Bisque Heads

each 8" (20 cm.) Each has bisque socket head with sculpted hair and facial features, all wooden articulated body with slits in hands and feet for positioning. Included are: Lady Acrobat with original costume trimmed in gold metallic rick-rack; Gentleman Acrobat with brown hair and moustache (costume not original); another Gentleman Acrobat with brown hair and moustache with original costume trimmed with metallic gold edging; Lion Tamer with brown hair and moustache, original costume and hat; and Ringmaster with black hair, moustache and goatee, original costume and hat. Excellent condition of all. Schoenhut, circa 1915. $1500/2000

Cherries Jubilee

139. German Bisque Pouty, 6969, by Gebruder Heubach
13" (33 cm.) Pink-tinted bisque socket head, blue glass sleep eyes, painted lashes, short feathered brows, accented nostrils and eye corners, closed mouth with center accent line, brunette mohair wig, composition and wooden ball-jointed body. Condition: generally excellent. Marks: 6969 3 Germany. Comments: Gebruder Heubach, circa 1912. Value Points: dear character with wistful expression, fine quality bisque, antique folklore costume, original body with original finish. $1600/1900

140. American Wooden Cart "St. Claus, Dealer in Good Things" and Horse
23" (59 cm.) A red wooden stake cart with yellow stenciling and yellow spoked wheels has sign "St. Claus, Dealer in Good Things" on its side, and is being pulled by a flannel covered paper mache horse with glass eyes, fancy harness, mounted upon a wheeled wooden base. Excellent condition. Circa 1890. $900/1300

141. Two Felix the Cat Toys by Schoenhut
3 1/2" and 8". Each is all wooden with ball-shaped head having white mask painted face and googly eyes, wooden-segmented limbs and tails for articulation, leather ears. Condition: generally excellent. Marks: Felix. Copyright 1922-1924 by Pat. Sullivan. Pat. Applied for. Comments: Schoenhut, circa 1925. Value Points: early cartoon figures are perfectly preserved. $500/600

143. German Paper Mache Mechanical Clown
9" (23 cm.) Paper mache oversized head with painted clown features and decorations, on carton torso that contains simple mechanical works that operate from key at back torso, wooden hands and feet. Condition: generally excellent, functions well. Comments: Germany, circa 1910, when wound the clown revolves and shakes in amusing manner. Value Points: perfectly preserved original condition including costume. $300/400

144. German Composition "Happy Hooligan" Doll
7" (18 cm.) Composition socket head with sculpted bald pate and red tin can hat, painted facial features with googly eyes and caricature wide beaming smile, composition five piece body, original black felt jacket and checkered pants. Condition: generally excellent. Comments: Happy Hooligan from early comic strip series, circa 1910, made in Germany. Value Points: rare little cartoon doll in wonderfully preserved condition. $400/500

145. German Bisque Character "Phillip" by Kammer and Reinhardt
16" (42 cm.) Bisque socket head, brown glass sleep eyes, painted lower lashes, short feathered brows, accented nostrils, closed mouth with downcast pouty expression on lips, chubby cheeks, double chin, brunette human hair, composition and wooden ball-jointed body with side-hip jointing. Condition: generally excellent. Marks: K*R Simon & Halbig115/A 42. Comments: Kammer and Reinhardt, "Phillip" from their art character series, circa 1912. Value Points: wonderful model of the pouty-faced fellow with very deeply sculpted features, finest quality of bisque, original toddler body with original finish, antique linen costume, knit cap, leather boots. $3800/4500

Cherries Jubilee

147. German Bisque Child by Kammer and Reinhardt
19 1/2" (50 cm.) Bisque socket head, brown glass eyes, painted lashes, dark eyeliner, short brush-stroked brows, accented eye corners, open mouth, shaded and accented lips, four porcelain teeth, pierced ears, blonde mohair wig, composition and wooden ball-jointed body. Condition: generally excellent. Marks: Simon & halbig K*R 50. Comments: Kammer and Reinhardt, circa 1915. Value Points: beautiful model of the classic dolly-face doll with choice bisque, original wig, body, body finish, wonderful antique costume. $700/900

148. Pair, German Bisque Dolls by Kammer and Reinhardt with Trunk and Trousseau
7 1/2" each doll. Each has bisque socket head, brown or blue glass sleep eyes, painted lashes, brush-stroked brows, open mouth, two teeth, blonde mohair wig, composition body with jointing at shoulders, hips and knees. Condition: generally excellent. Marks: K*R Halbig 19. Comments: Kammer and Reinhardt, circa 1915. Value Points: the twin dolls are presented in their original trunk with an assortment of costumes, some original to the trunk, others handmade. $1100/1500

146. German Bisque Toddler, 126, with Flirty Eyes by Kammer and Reinhardt
15" (36 cm.) Bisque socket head, blue glass sleep and "flirty" eyes, painted lashes, brush-stroked and feathered brows, accented nostrils and eye corners, open mouth, shaded and accented lips, two porcelain teeth, brunette mohair bobbed wig, composition and wooden ball-jointed toddler body with side-hip jointing, antique organdy costume, undergarments, socks. Condition: generally excellent. Marks: K*R Simon & Halbig Germany 32. Comments: Kammer and Reinhardt, circa 1918. Value Points: pretty toddler with fine matte bisque, well-functioning flirty eyes, in pristine unplayed with condition. $600/800

149. German Bisque Pouty Character, 115/A, by Kammer and Reinhardt
23" (60 cm.) Bisque socket head, blue glass sleep eyes, painted lashes, short feathered brows, accented nostrils of rounded nose, closed mouth with downcast lips, pouty expression, plump cheeks, blonde mohair wig, composition and wooden ball-jointed toddler body with side-hip jointing, wearing lavish antique costume of lace-trimmed whitewear dress and bonnet, undergarments, stockings, blue kidskin shoes. Condition: generally excellent. Marks: K*R Simon & Halbig 115/A 60. Comments: Kammer and Reinhardt, circa 1912, from their art character series. Value Points: superb original condition of the larger size of this model with choice bisque, dewy patina of complexion, rarer toddler body in original finish. $4000/5500

150. German Bisque "Mein Liebling" by Kammer and Reinhardt
21" (55 cm.) Bisque socket head, blue glass sleep eyes, dark eyeliner, painted lashes, short feathered brows, accented eye corners and nostrils, closed mouth with shaded and accented lips, blonde mohair wig, composition and wooden ball-jointed body. Condition: generally excellent. Marks: K*R Simon & Halbig 117 55. Comments: Kammer and Reinhardt, the gentle-featured model was a transitional doll between their art character series and classic dolly series, circa 1912. Value Points: most endearing expression is enhanced by fine quality of bisque and painting, original body and body finish, beautiful antique lace and rose cotton costume, undergarments, leather shoes. $4500/6500

Cherries Jubilee

151. French Bisque Bebe Schmitt in Rare Size
10 1/2" (27 cm.). Bisque socket head, blue glass enamel inset eyes with spiral threading, dark eyeliner, delicately painted lashes and brows, accented nostrils and eye corners, closed mouth with pale accented lips, pierced ears, blonde mohair wig. French composition and wooden body with eight-loose-ball-joints, straight wrists, shapely ankles and elongated slender feet, wearing antique lace edged muslin chemise. Condition: generally excellent. Marks: Sch (in shield, on head and body) 4/ 0 (head). Comments: Schmitt et Fils, circa 1882, the model has a slightly different look, transitional between the round moon face model and the pear-shaped face model. Value Points: most endearing little doll has beautiful face and bisque, original signed head and body, original body finish. $9000/13,000

152. Miniature Bisque Doll in Presentation Box for the French Market

4" doll. A bisque socket head doll with blue glass sleep eyes, painted lashes, and brows, open mouth, blonde mohair wig, five piece body with painted shoes and shoes and wearing a lace edged muslin chemise, is presented in a glass front display box with lace edging, along with her trousseau: rose silk dress, panties, hankie, cap, bebe stays, and cape, each lavishly trimmed with lace or rose silk ribbons. Marks: Halbig K*R 12 (doll) SFBJ (stylized lettering on paper label on base of box). Comments: for the French market, circa 1915. Value Points: wonderful presentation box with well-detailed original costumes, unplayed with condition, with rare original label. $1200/1800

153. Miniature Bisque Doll in Presentation Box for the French Market

4" doll. Identical to #152 except having brunette mohair wig and blue costumes and ribbons. Marks: Halbig K*R 12 (doll) SFBJ (stylized lettering on paper label on base of box). Comments: for the French market, circa 1915. Value Points: rare presentation box in wonderfully preserved with dainty and detailed original antique costumes. $1200/1800

154. Splendid French Bisque Bebe by Petit et Dumoutier

22" (56 cm.) Pressed bisque socket head with rounded facial modeling, large blue glass paperweight inset eyes with out rich spiral threading, thick black eyeliner, painted lashes, brush-stroked and feathered brows, accented eye corners, shaded nostrils, closed mouth with shaded and accented lips, pierced ears, brunette human hair wig. French composition and wooden body with eight-loose-ball joints, metal hands. Condition: generally excellent, some retouch to fingers. Marks: P. 4 D. Comments: Petit et Dumoutier, circa 1884. Value Points: rare bebe in wonderful large size with unusually pretty face, choice bisque, beautiful eyes, original body, lovely antique dress, undergarments, leather shoes. $8000/12,000

155. French Bisque Polichinelle in Original Costume

15" (38 cm.) Bisque head with bright blue eyes, painted lashes and brows, accented nostrils, closed mouth with accented lips, blonde mohair wig, on block torso with shaped humps at front and back torso, bisque hands, paper mache lower legs with shaped upturned toes on shoes. Condition: generally excellent. Comments: Polichinelle, the popular French figure of stories and legends in the 19th century; several French firms specialized in creating dolls of this popular figure, circa 1890. Value Points: wonderfully preserved example wearing his original rose and aqua Polichinelle costume and hat trimmed with gold metallic fringe and braid, little bells. $2000/2500

Cherries Jubilee

156. Vintage Photograph Print of Young Girl with Bebe Jumeau
25" x 38" framed. 11" x 23" image. A photograph print of a pretty young girl holding her doll, that is clearly a Bebe Jumeau, is enhanced with varnish touches (rehausee) and pen dated on the bottom of the photograph 1904, antique frame. $700/900

157. French Terra Cotta Statue of Young Girl Holding a Doll
20" (51 cm.) Terra cotta sculpture of young girl with down-tiled head gazing at her cherished doll that she holds in her arms; the girl has hair ribbon and bow, ruffled dress of the 1880 era, buckled shoes, and is standing upon a self base that is signed "Mage". French. circa 1885. Excellent condition. $800/1100

158. French Faience Plate with Doll Store Image
8" diameter. A soft paste faience plate is trimmed with lavish border that centers a scene of woman offering dolls and toys for sale at the shop "Au Tambour Rouge". Included in the scene are dolls, drums, Polichinelle and wagons. Impressed P&B Choisy on reverse. French,

circa 1840. A rare plate with doll theme is wonderfully detailed. Excellent condition. $600/900

159. French Porcelain Plate "Au Paradis des Enfant"
7 1/2" diameter. Porcelain plate with black and white elaborate border centering an image of well-dressed gentleman in top hat leaving a street stall labeled "Au Paradis des Enfant". his arms laden with dolls. Polichinelle. rocking horse and a box of bon-bons. Two other people are standing at the stall that is still laden with toys. The plate is labeled "Etrennes", and signed on reverse "Poterie J. Viellard". Excellent condition. Circa 1860. $600/800

160. A Beautiful French Bisque Bebe Schmitt
25" (64 cm.) Pressed bisque socket head with pear-shaped facial modeling. blue glass paperweight inset eyes of great depth. dark eyeliner. brush-stroked and multi-feathered brows. mauve blushed eye shadow. accented eye corners. shaded nostrils. distinctive pointy-tip nose. closed mouth with heart-shaped upper lip. defined space between the outlined lips. plump cheeks and chin. pierced ears. brunette mohair wig over cork pate. French composition and wooden eight-loose-ball-jointed body with straight wrists and curled fingers. flat-cut derriere. Condition: generally excellent. Marks: Sch (shield mark on head and torso). Comments: Schmitt et Fils. circa 1884. Value Points: beautiful wide-eyed bebe has lovely bisque and painting. original signed body. lavish antique costume of dotted Swiss with ruffled bonnet. multi-layered undergarments including bebe corset. leather shoes. socks. $10.000/13.000

161. French Miniature Glass Dome with Silk Flowers
9" (23 cm.) Tall blown glass dome on original wooden base encloses an arrangement of white silk flowers and green leaves within a white Porcelain de Paris vase decorated with a garland of blue flowers and gilt edging. French. circa 1880. Excellent condition. A rare small size of the popular parlor decoration. perfectly sized for doll display. $300/400

Cherries Jubilee

162. Antique French Silk Costume and Jewelry
28"l. 10" shoulders. Of aqua silk with black velvet trim, patterned silk blouse with aqua silk plastron and Alencon lace, clusters of wax orange blossoms and delicate flowers and leaves, with matching lace-edged apron. Along with gold-finished bracelet clasp and bangle earrings. Excellent condition, water spot on apron. French, circa 1880. A rare and beautifully preserved early costume. $600/900

Detail. #162.

163. French Sewing Necessaire in Book Shape
5" x 3 1/2". A firm-sided box in the shape of a book with embossed designs and title, opens to reveal hollowed interior lined with purple velvet and fitted with miniature sewing tools such as gold needlecase, gold thimble, scissors, needs, bone tools, mirror, three little boxes with engravings, thread. French, circa 1870. Excellent condition. $500/700

164. German Sample Card of Buckles
11" x 6 1/2". A heavy card features 29 silver or gold buckles in different designs, along with original inventory numbers, the card is written in German and English. circa 1890. Along with an ivory silk twill pillow with exquisite embroidery and silk flowers, embroidered silk chiffon ruffles at each corner. $400/500

Cherries Jubilee

165. French Miniature Lace-Making Board
6 1/2" x 6". Firm-sided form with checkerboard patterns and silk ribbons is fitted with original paper pattern, pins, and ten wooden bobbins with original paper wrappings, a child-sized version of the adult lace-making board, perfect for doll display. In fine unused condition. French, circa 1900. $400/600

166. Outstanding French Bisque Bebe Schmitt in Grand Size
31" (79 cm.) Pressed bisque socket head with pear-shaped facial modeling and very plump cheeks, almond-shaped blue glass enamel inset eyes with spiral threading and great depth, dark eyeliner, delicately painted lashes, mauve blushed eye shadow, widely arched feathered brows, accented eye corners, shaded nostrils, closed mouth with defined white space between the shaded and outlined lips, dimpled blushed chin, pierced blushed ears, blonde lambswool wig over cork pate, French composition and wooden eight-loose-ball-jointed body with straight wrists, antique silk dress, undergarments, aqua cashmere woolen coat with cape having quilted lining and cutwork edging, silk cap, red leather shoes. Condition: generally excellent. Marks: Sch (head and derriere) 8 (head). Comments: Schmitt et Fils, circa 1882. Value Points: outstanding grand bebe from the illustrious firm with finest quality of pale bisque enhanced by rich painting, original body and body finish, splendid costume. $16,000/22,000

167. French Child's Cherrywood Spinning Wheel
25" (64 cm.) Of rich cherrywood with natural finish, the spinning wheel features beautifully spindles and details. Excellent condition. Circa 1880. $300/400

Cherries Jubilee

168. French Doll in Elaborate Jester Costume
35" (89 cm.) Early celluloid head with blue glass paperweight eyes, mohair lashes encircle the eyes, incised eyeliner, feathered brows, closed mouth with smiling expression, dimpled lip corners, brunette human hair wig, hand-made muslin body with composition hands. Condition: generally excellent. Marks: SG France 64. Comments: the 1880-era costume is displayed on handmade form and doll head of 1915 era. Value Points: wonderful presentation, with elaborate black velvet jester's costume lavishly trimmed with aqua silk ribbons and lace edging, aqua silk cap with silver bells, black velvet shoes. $900/1200

169. Very Fine French Doll's Dinner Service in Original Box
18" x 14" box closed. 5"w. tureen. A firm-sided wooden box is covered with white floral pattern and opens in an elaborate manner to reveal pale blue paper lined interior with pink edging, multi-tiered arrangement with cream softpaste dinner service decorated with embossed green-stemmed blue wildflowers and gilt borders; the service comprising lidded soup tureen, lidded bowl, open bowl, two footed compotes, gravy boat, two round serving plates, two oval serving plates, two small plates, three relish dishes, two enamel glass etageres, two decanters, wooden framed cruet holder with two glass cruets with stoppers, four soup bowls, four plates, four gold-plated knives, forks and spoons, four silver knife rests, three glass goblets, four menus, one serving spoon, and four silver napkin rings, still tied inside box with original blue ribbons. Excellent condition, one plate reglued, one bowl has hairline. French, circa 1885, a superb and remarkably preserved dinner service of luxury quality. $900/1300

170. German Bisque Asian Child with Elaborate Costume for the French Market
16" doll. (41 cm.) Amber tinted bisque socket head, brown glass inset eyes, black painted lashes, black feathered brows, accented nostrils and eye corners, open mouth, outlined lips, four porcelain teeth, pierced ears, black human hair in elaborate coiffure, amber tinted body with ball-jointed elbows, one piece legs. Condition: generally excellent. Marks: 1329 Germany Simon & Halbig S&H 4. Comments: Simon and Halbig for the French market, circa 1895. Value Points: the beautiful doll wears her elaborate original Asian costume comprising elaborate head dress enwrapping her hair, silk costume, shoes with wooden heels, tassels. $2000/2500

171. *French Bisque Bebe EJ by Jumeau, Size 9*
19" (48 cm.) Pressed bisque socket head, large brown glass paperweight inset eyes, dark eyeliner, painted lashes, brush-stroked and multi-feathered brows, rose blushed eye shadow, accented eye corners, shaded nostrils, closed mouth with defined space between the shaded and accented lips, separately modeled pierced ears, blonde mohair wig over cork pate. French composition and wooden fully-jointed body with straight wrists. Condition: generally excellent. Marks: E.8 J. (and artist check marks) Jumeau Medaille d'Or Paris (body stamp). Comments: Emile Jumeau, circa 1885. Value Points: gorgeous bebe with finest quality bisque and dramatic large brown eyes, original body and body finish, wig, pate, antique aqua silk dress, undergarments, lace bonnet with aqua ribbons, black leather shoes signed E.J., Jumeau socks. $7500/9500

Cherries Jubilee

172. French Bisque Automaton "Little Boy with Basket of Flowers and Bee" by Lambert

18" (46 cm.) Standing upon a maroon velvet covered base is a bisque-head boy with blue glass paperweight inset eyes, lushly painted lashes, wide brushstroked brows, closed mouth with accented lips, pierced ears, brunette mohair wig over cork pate, carton torso and legs, wire upper arms, bisque forearms, wearing cavalier costume of ivory and rose silk, black silk hat, and carrying a woven basket of silk flowers in which a bee is perched. When wound, music plays, the boy turns his head from side to side, then lifts the bouquet of flowers he holds in his right hand while the bee in the basket flits around as though to gather honey from the flowers. Condition: generally excellent. Marks: Depose Tete Jumeau 3 (doll) LB (key) La Czarine (and another illegible title, two tunes on paper label on base with LB label). Comments: Leopold Lambert, circa 1888. Value Points: wonderfully amusing activity of busy bee, merrily-costumed lad, two tunes with original label. $7500/9500

173. Eleven French Soft Paste Plates "Theatre Guignol"

each 8" (20 cm.) Each of fine creamy soft paste with blue patterned border centering a scene from Theatre Guignol, the popular puppet theatre of 19th century France; each is a different scene from one of the puppet theatre plays presented during that time, including Romeo and Juliet, If I was King, Around the World, and others. Marked MBCM, Montereau, Made in France. Excellent condition, one with two rim chips. A rare set with wonderful detail. France, circa 1880. $1100/1500

174. An Outstanding French Leather Poupee in Original Costume

23" (58 cm.) Mold-pressed leather doll has aristocratic appearance, separately formed head with socket neck, aquiline nose, cut-out eye sockets with inset glazed eyes, stitched pierced ears, elongated throat, elaborately coiffed hair, stitched seam shapely body with modeled bosom, tiny waist, stitched and separated long fingers. Condition: generally excellent, tiny nose tip wear. Comments: France, circa 1875, the maker is unknown although a smaller version of the doll was shown in L'Illustration magazine toward the end of the century in a famous exhibition of French dolls. Value Points: extremely rare doll of outstanding beauty, regal presentation, intricate construction, wearing original ivory silk taffeta gown with lace, pearl beads, and metallic trim, elaborately wrapped turban, gold gold earrings and necklace, still preserved in her original wooden box. $6000/9500

Cherries Jubilee

175. German Mohair Teddy by Steiff
12" (31 cm.) Golden mohair teddy with excelsior filling, swivel head, stitched ears, long snout nose, hump back, elongated jointed disc arms, hip-jointed legs, felt paws, brown embroidered nose tip, shoe-button eyes, original silver Steiff button in ear. Excellent condition. Steiff, circa 1915. $1200/1500

176. German Bisque Toddler, 1295, by Franz Schmidt
8" (20 cm.) Bisque socket head, brown glass sleep eyes, painted lashes, short feathered brows, accented eye corners, pierced nostrils, open mouth, two teeth, blonde mohair bobbed wig, composition five piece toddler body with side-hip jointing. Condition: generally excellent. Marks: 1295 F.S. & C. made in Germany. Comments: Franz Schmidt, circa 1915. Value Points: wonderful little toddler with pristine body, appealing expression and fine bisque. $600/800

177. German Bisque Child by Kestner
19" (48 cm.) Bisque socket head, blue glass sleep eyes, painted lashes, dark eyeliner, brush-stroked and feathered brows, accented eye corners and nostrils, open mouth, shaded and accented lips, two porcelain upper teeth, blonde mohair wig over plaster pate, composition and wooden ball-jointed body. Condition: generally excellent. Marks: G made in Germany 11 (head) Germany (body). Comments: Kestner, circa 1900, their 143 model. Value Points: most appealing dolly-face model with original wig, pate, body, body finish, lovely antique costume. $700/900

178. German Bisque Child, 152, by Kestner
16" (41 cm.) Bisque socket head, brown glass sleep eyes, painted lashes, feathered brows, accented nostrils and eye corners, open mouth, outlined lips, four teeth, blonde mohair wig over plaster pate, composition and wooden ball-jointed body. Condition: generally excellent. Marks: C Made in Germany 152 7 (head) Germany (body). Comments: Kestner, circa 1900. Value Points: pretty child doll, a more rarely found model, has original body, body finish, wig, pate, antique costume. $700/900

179. German Bisque Closed Mouth Child by Kestner
12" (31 cm.) Bisque socket head. brown glass sleep eyes. painted lashes. brush-stroked brows. accented eye corners and nostrils. closed mouth with accented lips. blonde mohair wig over plaster pate. composition and wooden eight-loose-ball-jointed body with straight wrists. nicely costumed. Condition: generally excellent. early body repaint. Marks: 7. Comments: Kestner. circa 1890. Value Points: appealing petite model of the early closed mouth child with fine bisque and sculpting. $1300/1800

180. German All-Bisque Doll Attributed to Kestner
8 1/2" (22 cm.) Bisque swivel head with squared jaw. blue glass inset eyes, painted lashes, feathered brows. rose eye shadow. accented eye corners and nostrils. open mouth with slightly parted lips, two square cut upper teeth, one square cut lower tooth, pierced ears. blonde mohair wig. peg-jointed bisque arms modeled bent at the elbows. side-hip jointed legs with musculature detail. tiny ankles. black heeled five strap shoes. lace dress. Condition: generally excellent. tiny chips on hip rim of legs. Marks: 102 12. Comments: attributed to Kestner. circa 1890. Value Points: rare model in fine large size with beautiful detail of modeling and bisque. $1200/1800

181. German Bisque Child, 129, by Kestner
13" (33 cm.) Bisque socket head. brown glass sleep eyes. painted lashes. brush-stroked and feathered brows. accented nostrils and eye corners. open mouth. outlined lips. blonde mohair wig over plaster pate. composition and wooden ball-jointed body. antique dress and undergarments. Condition: generally excellent. Marks: C made in Germany 7 129 (head) Excelsior (body). Comments: Kestner. circa 1900. a hard to find model with wonderful expression. original wig. pate. body. body finish. $700/900

Cherries Jubilee

182. Large German Bisque Child, 171, by Kestner
32" (81 cm.) Bisque socket head, brown glass sleep eyes, thick painted eye liner, painted lashes, slightly modeled brush-stroked and feathered brows with decorative glaze, accented eye corners and nostrils, open mouth, accented lips, four porcelain teeth, pierced ears, blonde mohair wig over plaster pate, composition and wooden ball-jointed body, antique whitewear costume, undergarments, socks, shoes. Condition: generally excellent. Marks: 16 1/2 made in Germany 16 _ 171 7 (head) Excelsior Germany (body). Comments: Kestner, circa 1900. Value Points: beautiful dolly-face model has choice bisque, original wig, pate, body, body finish. $900/1200

182A. Large German All Bisque Figure by Gebruder Heubach
16" (41 cm.) One piece bisque figurine depicting a laughing girl with blonde curly hair beneath a ruffled sunbonnet, wearing green dress with rose petal design and pink bodice, posed upon a bisque self-base as though about to skip rope. Gebruder Heubach, circa 1900, with fabulous detail of sculpting of face dimples and costume folds. $900/1300

183. German Bisque Child, 167, by Kestner
21" (54 cm.) Bisque socket head, blue glass sleep eyes, painted lashes, brush-stroked modeled brows with decorative glaze, dark eyeliner, painted lashes, accented nostrils and eye corners, open mouth with accented lips, four porcelain teeth, blonde mohair wig over plaster pate, composition and wooden ball-jointed body. Condition: generally excellent. Marks: made in Germany 10 1/2 167 Germany. Comments: Kestner, circa 1900. Value Points: beautiful gleaming complexion enhances the wide-eyed expression, original body and body finish, lovely antique costume. $800/1000

184. German Bisque Child with Closed Mouth, Model 169, by Kestner
20" (51 cm.) Bisque socket head, brown glass sleep eyes, painted lashes, slightly modeled brush-stroked brows with decorative glaze, accented eye corners and nostrils, closed mouth with shaded lips, brunette mohair wig over plaster pate. Condition: generally excellent. Marks: F. made in Germany 10 169. Comments: Kestner, circa 1900. Value Points: closed mouth child with lovely bisque, antique dress, undergarments, rose shoes and stockings, bonnet. $1200/1600

185. German Bisque Child, 143, by Kestner
13" (33 cm.) Bisque socket head, blue glass sleep eyes, painted lashes, incised eyeliner, feathered brows, accented nostrils, open mouth, shaded and accented lips, two porcelain teeth, blonde mohair wig over plaster pate, composition and wooden ball-jointed body. Condition: generally excellent. Marks: C made in

Germany 7 143 (head) Germany (body). Comments: Kestner, circa 1910. Value Points: wonderful girl with expressive features, original wig, pate, body, body finish, antique costume cap, shoes, undergarments. $700/900

186. German Bisque Miniature Doll in Surprise Egg
3" (8 cm.) Bisque socket head, blue glass eyes, open mouth, mohair wig, five piece composition body with painted shoes and socks, silk dress; the little girl is arranged inside a woven egg-shaped basket along with a variety of tiny accessories tied onto three additional cards, including little toys, costumes, toiletries, school bag and jump rope. Excellent condition. French, circa 1890. A rare presentation of the little surprise doll with her possessions. $800/1000

187. German Bisque Child, 1249, by Simon and Halbig
14" (36 cm.) Bisque socket head, blue glass sleep eyes, painted lashes, brush-stroked brows with feathered details, accented nostrils and eye corners, open mouth, accented lips, four porcelain teeth, pierced ears, blonde mohair wig, composition and wooden ball-jointed body. Condition: generally excellent. Marks: S&H 1249 Dep Germany 4 1/2. Comments: Simon and Halbig, circa 1900. Value Points: beautiful cabinet size doll has lovely bisque, characteristic accent dot on bottom lip, original body and body finish, antique lace dress, straw bonnet, undergarments, stockings, black leatherette shoes. $800/1000

188. German All-Bisque Doll with High Grey Stockings
8" (20 cm.) Bisque swivel head on kid-edged bisque torso, brown glass sleep eyes, painted lashes, single stroke brows, accented nostrils, closed mouth, blonde mohair wig, peg-jointed bisque arms and slender legs with grey painted stockings to above the knees, brown one-strap shoes, antique crocheted costume and cap. Condition: generally excellent. Marks: 1079 Halbig S&H Germany 3/0. Comments: Simon and Halbig, circa 1900. Value Points: rarity factors include swivel head, grey stockings, closed mouth. $800/1100

Cherries Jubilee

189. Grand French Bisque Poupee Attributed to Barrois
30" (76 cm.) Pale bisque shoulderhead with rounded facial modeling, cobalt blue glass enamel inset eyes, dark eyeliner, painted lashes, lightly feathered brows, accented nostrils and eye corners, closed mouth with accented lips, pierced ears, brunette human hair over cork pate, kid fashion body with shapely torso, gusset-jointed limbs, antique bronze silk costume with brown taffeta trim, matching bonnet. Condition: generally excellent.. Comments: attributed to Barrois, circa 1865. Value Points: fine large exhibition size poupee with brilliant eyes complementing the delicate bisque. $3500/4500

190. French Terra Cotta Figure of Young Child by Albert Marque
11" h. (28 cm.) One piece terra cotta sculpture with bronzed-color finish of young child with curly hair, chubby dimpled body, seated on knoll, holding one hand to mouth, the other holding his foot. Signed "No.2. Albert Marque", in the classic signature of the artist. French, circa 1915, from the artist who also designed the classic Albert Marque doll during the same era. A rare sculpture with appealing subject. $2000/2500

191. French Bisque Poupee Attributed to Jumeau
17" (45 cm.) Bisque swivel head on kid-edged bisque shoulder plate, cobalt blue glass enamel inset eyes, painted

Cherries Jubilee

lashes, lightly feathered brows, accented nostrils, closed mouth with accented lips, pierced ears, brunette mohair wig over cork pate, kid fashion body with gusset jointing, wearing green silk gown of vintage fabrics. Condition: generally excellent, very faint hairline on front shoulder plate. Comments: attributed to Jumeau, circa 1875. Value Points: beautiful face on the lady fashion doll with brilliant eyes, soft complexion. $1200/1700

192. Early Model French Bisque Bebe by Gaultier

19" (48 cm.) Pale pressed bisque swivel head on kid-edged bisque shoulder plate, blue glass enamel inset eyes with rich spiral threading, dark thick eyeliner, painted lashes, mauve blushed eye shadow, widely arched feathered brows, accented eye corners and nostrils, closed mouth with shaded and accented lips, pierced ears, brunette human hair over cork pate, French kid bebe body with gusset jointing, bisque forearms with nicely shaped fingers, antique green silk bronze frock, undergarments, leather shoes, blue stockings, fancy straw bonnet. Condition: generally excellent, right baby finger missing. Marks: F. 8 G. (block letters) Comments: Gaultier, circa 1882. Value Points: rare earliest model of the Gaultier bebe with original kid bebe body, lovely pale bisque. $6000/7500

193. French Walnut Doll's Cupboard with Soft Paste Dinnerware

28"h. (71 cm.) Of rich dark walnut, in the manner of Southern France, the cupboard features open-shelved top, counter, and a base with three drawers flanked by a pair of glass-front doors. The cupboard crest and sides are decorated with decorative panels. Included are a lot of soft paste cream ware dishes decorated with country scenes. Circa 1875. $800/1000

Cherries Jubilee

194. French Bisque Automaton "The Dandy" by Lambert
24" overall. Standing upon a velvet covered base is a bisque-headed doll with blue glass eyes, dramatic eye decoration, brush-stroked brows, accented nostrils and eye corners, open mouth, shaded and accented lips, four porcelain teeth, pierced ears, brunette human hair, long slender torso and legs of carton, wire upper arms, bisque forearms, costumed in rich silk and brocades as a fancy Court dandy. When wound, he turns his head from side to side, nods forward, blinks his eyes, and alternately lifts the walking stick in his right arm, and the rich gilt lorgnette in his left hand. Condition: generally excellent, old faint hairline at back of head, mechanism and music function well. Marks: 1159 Germany Simon & Halbig 6 (doll) LB (key) (original paper label lists two tunes, "Valencia" and "Oh mademoiselle"). Comments: Leopold Lambert, circa 1895. Value Points: wonderfully appealing automaton whose pose and costume and perfectly suited to his actions and music. $4500/6500

195. Very Rare French Bisque Head for Milliner by Bru
15" (38 cm.) to base. 10"l (25 cm.) head. The human-sized bisque head has very slender facial modeling and elongated strong throat, blue glass paperweight inset eyes, dark eyeliner, painted lashes with dot highlights, brush-stroked and multi-fringed brows, rose blushed eye shadow, aquiline nose with shaded nostrils, accented eye corners, closed mouth with shaded and outlined lips, pierced ears, strong chin with dimpled detail, brunette human hair over cork pate, antique lambswool cap. The head is dowel-mounted (removable) upon original ebony wooden platform. Condition: generally excellent. Marks: B. Bru No. 3. Comments: Bru, circa 1890. Bru Jne & Cie produced a very exclusive line of bisque heads, on commission, for the display windows of coiffeurs, milliners and jewelers. Value Points: very rare signed milliner's head by the Bru firm with rare original stand, very fine quality of bisque and painting with portrait-like expression. $9000/13,000

196. French Puzzles in Original Box
15" x 11". A set of heavy cardboard jig-saw puzzles with beautiful lithographed scenes of life in Paris and the French countryside; included are three puzzles, each able to be removed separately from the original presentation box by means of silk ribbons. In near pristine condition. French, circa 1885, with lithographs by H. Sicard, 28 rue Amelot, Paris. $800/1000

197. Very Rare German Bisque Character, 1307, by Simon and Halbig in Grand Size
23" (59 cm.) Bisque socket head, dark brown glass sleep eyes, dark eyeliner, heavily modeled eyelids, painted lashes, slightly modeled brush-stroked and feathered brows, accented eye corners and shaded nostrils, closed mouth with accent line between the lips, brunette mohair wig, French composition and wooden fully jointed body, antique blue woolen suit with soutache trim, white shirt, tricorn hat, black stockings and shoes. Condition: generally excellent. Marks: 1307 11. Comments: Simon and Halbig, circa 1900, body appears original suggesting the production of the doll for the French market. Value Points: extremely rare model in fine larger size with superb bisque, modeling and painting, few examples of this doll are known to exist. $15,000/21,000

Cherries Jubilee

199. German All-Bisque Mignonette
7" (17 cm.) Bisque swivel head on kid-edged bisque torso, brown glass sleep eyes, painted lashes, arched feathered brows, accented nostrils and eye corners, open mouth, slightly parted lips, two square cut upper teeth, one square lower tooth, blonde mohair wig, peg-jointed bisque arms and legs, painted high blue stockings, black one strap shoes, antique dress. Condition: generally excellent, tiny chip at top of back torso. Comments: Simon and Halbig, circa 1890. Value Points: fine larger size all-bisque with swivel head, pretty face. $800/1000

198. French Walnut Doll's Sewing Cupboard with Sewing Machine
23" (58 cm.) Walnut armoire mirrored double front doors has fancily carved crest and apron, and an elaborately fitted interior comprising tin and cast iron toy sewing machine, bobbins, bone sewing tools, samples, lace, threads, and other accessories for teaching needlework to a young child. A remarkable and well-preserved early toy as seen in French department store Etrennes catalogs. French, circa 1890. $1200/1800

200. French Candy Container "Little Girl in a Shoe"
8"l. (20 cm.) A paper mache candy container in the shape of a sabot style shoe has a maroon silk sack protruding from the top, and a bisque head, bisque arms and bisque bare feet, protruding from five cut-outs in the shoe as though the doll is bursting out. The cutouts are edged with red velvet. French, circa 1885. $700/900

201. German Bisque Child in Labeled Nurse's Uniform

23" (58 cm.) Bisque socket head. blue glass sleep eyes. painted lashes. dark eyeliner. brush-stroked and feathered brows. accented nostrils and eye corners. open mouth. shaded and accented lips. four porcelain teeth. brunette human hair. composition and wooden ball-jointed body. Condition: generally excellent. Marks: 109 – 10 1/2 dep Germany Handwerck (head) Heinrich Handwerck (body). Comments: Handwerck. circa 1900. Value Points: in fine unplayed with condition. the doll wears original turn of the century Red Cross uniform comprising blue and white striped dress. apron. undergarments. striped blue and white wool stockings. black shoes. and heavy blue woolen double-breasted coat with velvet Cross on sleeve. and matching cape with original label "Armstrong Uniforms. Chicago Trademark". $900/1200

202. German Bisque Fashion Lady in Simon and Halbig

19" (48 cm.) Bisque socket head with slender facial modeling. blue glass sleep eyes. mohair lashes. painted lower lashes. feathered brows. accented nostrils. open mouth. shaded and accented lips. four porcelain teeth. pierced ears. brunette mohair wig in upswept style. composition and wooden ball-jointed body with adult female shape. modeled bosom. tiny waist. slender limbs. Condition: generally excellent. Marks: 1159 S&H DEP 7 Germany. Comments: Simon and Halbig. circa 1900. Value Points: in fine unplayed with condition. the lady wears her antique well-fitted uniform of blue and white striped dress. apron. cap. black leather shoes and stockings. $1200/1800

203. German Bisque Fashion Lady in Simon and Halbig

19" (48 cm.) Bisque socket head with slender facial modeling. blue glass sleep eyes. mohair lashes. painted lower lashes. feathered brows. accented nostrils. open mouth. shaded and accented lips. four porcelain teeth. pierced ears. blonde mohair wig in upswept style. composition and wooden ball-jointed body with adult female shape. modeled bosom. tiny waist. slender limbs. lingerie. Condition: generally excellent. Marks: 1159 S&H DEP 7 Germany. Comments: Simon and Halbig. circa 1900. Value Points: very beautiful doll in pristine condition. original wig. lashes. body with beautiful original finish. $1200/1800

204. Antique Metal Folding Doll Bed

10"h. folded. 23"l. An iron bed with fancy scroll designs and original metal springs. is designed to be folded when not in use. or to open flat and be moved about on tiny cast iron wheels. Uniquely sized for doll play. it is likely that piece was originally created for use as salesman's sample. Circa 1890. $800/1000

Cherries Jubilee

205. French Bisque Poupee by Leon Casimir Bru with Wooden Arms
19" (48 cm.) Bisque swivel head on kid-edged bisque shoulder plate, blue glass enamel inset eyes, dark eyeliner, painted lashes, brush-stroked brows, accented nostrils and eye corners, closed mouth with richly accented lips, ears pierced into head, brunette mohair wig over cork pate, firmly stuffed kid fashion torso and gusset-jointed legs, dowel-jointed wooden arms with jointing at shoulders, elbows and wrists, separately sculpted fingers, wearing antique lingerie including fancy red corset, red slippers. Condition: generally excellent. Marks: H. Comments: Leon Casimir Bru, circa 1867. Value Points: rare early Bru poupee with classic letter marking and deposed Bru body style, in fine large size with remarkable modeling of face; the model preceded the deposed smiling model. #206. $3000/4000

206. Splendid French Bisque Poupee with Smiling Expression by Leon Casimir Bru
28" (71 cm.) Bisque swivel head on kid-edged bisque shoulder plate, almond-shaped blue glass enamel inset eyes, dark eyeliner, painted lashes, widely arched brush-stroked and feathered brows, accented nostrils of aquiline nose, closed mouth with pale accented lips and hint of smile, blushed cheeks and eye shadow, pierced ears, blonde mohair wig over cork pate, French kid poupee body with shapely waist, square cut kid collarette, gusset-jointing at

elbows, hips and knees, stitched and separated fingers, antique costume comprising lovely white pique jacket with soutache trim, skirt, undergarments, lace cap with frou-frou ribbons, stockings, leather boots. Condition: generally excellent. Marks: M (head and shoulder plate) Depose M (forehead). Comments: Leon Casimir Bru, circa 1872, the year that the model was deposed by Bru. Value Points: very rare large size of the uniquely sculpted model with choice bisque and painting, original body. $4500/5500

207. French Poupee Parasol Attributed to Huret

9" (23 cm.) Metal-handled parasol with yellow paint decorated with black striping, has original silk cover of blue and ivory striped pattern, with silk fringe, ivory tip. The parasol is attributed to Huret, circa 1860. Excellent condition. $700/900

208. French Wooden Armoire for Linens and Cloths

25" (64 cm.) Painted white wooden armoire with bronze mounted decorations of cherubs and garlands centering a cameo like design has mirrored door, opens to reveal well-fitted interior with three shelves packed with table covers, doll bed linens, and homespun towels, all tied with original red silk ribbons, with lock and key. Excellent condition. French, circa 1890, perfectly scaled for display with 15"-20" dolls. $700/1000

209. French Bisque Bebe Schmitt, Size 2, with Boutique Label

17" (45 cm.) Bisque socket head with rounded facial modeling, blue glass inset eyes with spiral

threading, dark eyeliner, painted lashes, widely arched feathered brows, accented eye corners and nostrils, closed mouth with accented lips, pierced ears, blonde mohair wig over original Schmitt pate. French composition and wooden eight-loose-ball-jointed body with flat-cut derriere and straight wrists, nicely costumed. Condition: generally excellent. Marks: Bte SGDG 2 (head) Sch (body) A La Tentation, 72 Passage Vendome, Paris (body label). Comments: Schmitt et Fils, circa 1880. Value Points: lovely bebe with artistic painting that enhances the plump pale face, original body and body finish, rare original boutique label. $8500/11,500

Cherries Jubilee

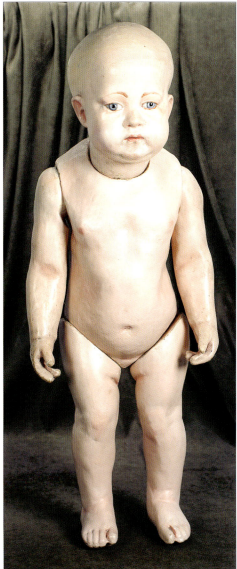

210. Very Rare and Superb Early French Paper Mache Bebe with Character Face
23" (59 cm.) Paper mache socket head with deeply impressed character features of solemn-faced child, solid dome, blue glass enamel inset eyes with spiral threading, painted lashes, rose blushed eye shadow, brush-stroked brows, accented eye corners and nostrils, closed mouth with shaded lips, brunette mohair wig, five piece paper mache toddler body with side-hip jointing, well-detailed musculature, antique muslin and

lace costume with woven bourrelet cap, slippers. Condition: generally excellent. Comments: early period bebe in the style of first bebes created by Jumeau and Schmitt, circa 1875, prior to bisque production: the dolls are discussed in The Jumeau Book, page 73, although this example has exceptional characterization, including detail of sculpted ears, mouth and around the eyes. Value Points: extremely rare doll whose value is enhanced by its great appeal and original condition. $7000/9500

210A. French Lambswool Pull-Toy Goat on Wheels

16"l. (41 cm.) Firm-sided paper mache goat is generously covered in white fluffy lambswool except for his smooth face and legs, with green glass inset eyes, defined mouth and nostrils, leather ears, elaborately carved horns, wooden hooves, with pull-wire that causes the goat to bleat when pulled, posed upon cast iron wheeled base. French, circa 1870, an early model of pull toy in rare animal form. $1100/1500

211. French Bisque Premiere Bebe by Jumeau

12" (31 cm.) Pressed bisque socket head, blue glass enamel inset eyes with spiral threading, lightly painted lashes, brush-stroked brows, accented nostrils and eye corners, closed mouth with outlined lips, pierced ears, blonde mohair wig over cork pate. French composition and wooden fully jointed body with eight-loose-ball-joints. Condition: generally excellent. Marks: 5 (head) Jumeau Medaille d'Or Paris (body). Comments: Emile Jumeau, his first model bebe, circa 1878. Value Points: especially pretty shy-faced bebe with entrancing large eyes, fine bisque, original body, antique delicate cotton cutwork dress, undergarments, aqua silk bonnet, socks, white kidskin shoes signed Paris. $6000/8000

212. French Bisque Bebe Triste by Jumeau, Size 13

28" (71 cm.) Pressed bisque socket head, blue glass paperweight inset eyes, dark eyeliner, painted lashes, mauve blushed eye shadow, brush-stroked and multi-feathered brows, accented eye corners, shaded nostrils, closed mouth with defined space between the shaded and outlined lips, separately modeled pierced ears, blonde mohair wig over cork pate. French composition and wooden fully jointed body with plump limbs, straight wrists. Condition: generally excellent, very faint hairline high on forehead. Marks: 13 (head) Jumeau Medaille d'Or Paris (body). Comments: Emile Jumeau, circa 1884. Value Points: wonderful model of Bebe Triste with large luminous eyes, fine creamy bisque, antique blue silk frock with white wool plastron, cuffs and collar, undergarments including bebe corset, signed Jumeau shoes, socks, lace bonnet. $8500/11,500

213. Very Rare French Bisque Bebe by Steiner with Taufling Body
22" (56 cm.) Bisque swivel head on bisque breast plate, unusual solid dome and pate cut at very back of head, rounded facial modeling, dark eyeliner, painted lashes, rose blushed eye shadow, feathered brows, accented nostrils and eye corners, open mouth, shaded lips, two rows of tiny teeth, dimpled chin, brunette human hair, unique body construction with muslin midriff and upper arms and legs, and bisque shoulder plate, lower torso and hips, lower arms and lower legs, bisque bare feet, antique costume. Condition: generally excellent, right thumb reglued. Comments: Jules Steiner, one of his earliest bebes with distinctive body known variously as "Motschmann" type, or taufling or bisque limb baby, circa 1870. Value Points: the rarity of the model is rivaled by its splendid quality of bisque and painting, fine large size, bisque limbs. $4500/6000

214. Petite French Bisque Bebe by Steiner with Taufling Body
13" (33 cm.) Solid domed bisque shoulderhead, blue glass enamel inset eyes, delicately painted lashes and brows, rose eye shadow, accented nostrils and eye corners, closed mouth with accent line between the teeth, unique body construction with muslin midriff and upper arms and legs, and bisque shoulder plate, lower torso and hips, lower arms and lower legs, bisque bare feet, blonde mohair wig, antique lace baby dress. Condition: generally excellent. Comments: Jules Steiner, a petite model of his taufling baby inspired by the Japanese Ichimatsu baby shown at the 1855 London Exposition. Value Points: very rare early doll with most appealing expression, wonderful all-original body, circa 1870. $4000/5000

215. French Bebe Ensemble in Presentation Box
To fit bebe about 10". A long baby dress of white waffle weave cotton has elaborately constructed cutwork front panel and sides, with attached bib front and collar, along with matching baby jacket, presented in white card paper box with lithograph of baby on the cover. French, circa 1880. Excellent condition. $300/400

216. French Paper Mache Child by Schmitt et Fils
16" (41 cm.) Solid domed paper mache head with slight wax overcoat, flat-cut neck socket that attaches to body by protruding dowel from torso, blue glass enamel inset eyes, painted lashes, lightly feathered brows, closed mouth with center accent line, blonde mohair wig, composition and wooden fully jointed body with flat-cut derriere, eight loose ball joints, straight wrists. Condition: generally excellent. Comments: Schmitt et Fils, circa 1875, early bebe from that firm preceding their bisque bebes. Value Points: very rare model with dear expression, original body, possibly original green woolen dress with lace overlay and blue silk sash, undergarments, shoes, socks, bonnet. $2500/3500

217. Petite French Bisque Bebe Steiner from Early Period
10" (26 cm.) Bisque socket head with rounded facial modeling, tiny blue glass enamel inset eyes, painted lashes, feathered brows, accented nostrils and eye corners, closed mouth with accented lips, blonde mohair wig over Steiner pate. Steiner composition and wooden fully jointed body, antique dress, undergarments, silk woven cap, blue leather slippers. Condition: generally excellent, some early body repaint. Marks: 3/0. Comments: Jules Steiner, circa 1875. Value Points: very early bebe in most appealing and rare petite size with original body, lovely complexion. $4500/6500

218. French Bisque Bebe Steiner from Early Period
14" (35 cm.) Bisque socket head with round facial shape, blue glass enamel inset eyes with spiral threading, dark eyeliner, painted lashes, mauve blushed eye shadow, lightly feathered brows, accented nostrils and eye corners, open mouth with delicately accented pale lips, two rows of tiny teeth, pierced ears, blonde mohair wig over Steiner pate. Steiner composition fully-jointed body and straight wrists. Condition: generally excellent, some finger wear. Comments: Jules Steiner, circa 1875. Value Points: early model bebe by Steiner with most endearing expression, original body, superb antique costume including white kidskin shoes signed "Au Bebe Bon Marche". $5500/7500

Cherries Jubilee

219. Wonderful Early French Paper Mache Pierrot in Original Costume
31" (79 cm.) Paper mache socket head with character features, upturned nose, smiling expression, white complexion, brown glass enamel inset eyes with heavily modeled eyelids, painted lashes, thickly fringed brows, accented nostrils, dimpled cheeks, black painted pate with stockinette edging, all paper mache body jointed at shoulders, elbows and hips, painted white gloves with detail of seams. Condition: generally excellent. Comments: French, circa 1880. Value Points: wonderful and very glass-eyed character with original paint, painted gloves, and most elaborate original silk Pierrot costume with blue silk buttons, ties and ribboned ivory silk shoes, ruffled collar. $3500/4500

220. An All-Original French Bisque Poupee Attributed to Jumeau
12" (31 cm.) Bisque swivel head on kid-edged bisque shoulder plate, blue glass enamel inset eyes, painted lashes, lightly feathered brows, accented nostrils and eye corners, closed mouth with accented lips, pierced ears, blonde mohair wig over cork pate, shapely kid fashion body with tiny waist, shaped

Cherries Jubilee

limbs, stitched and separated fingers. Condition: generally excellent, body near mint except some wire rust on fingers. Marks: 0. Comments: attributed to Jumeau, circa 1875. Value Points: in fine unplayed with condition, the doll wears original elaborate costume of Normandy including coiffe, gown, blue silk apron, earrings, and gilt ormolu accessories including glasses, hair pins, brooch, and watch and fob. $3000/4000

221. Petite French Bisque Poupee in Original Costume

11" (28 cm.) Bisque swivel head on kid-edged bisque shoulder plate, blue glass enamel inset eyes, painted lashes, feathered brows, accented nostrils and eye corners, pierced ears, closed mouth with accented lips, blonde mohair wig over cork pate, French kid fashion body with tiny waist, one piece shapely arms and legs, stitched and separated fingers. Condition: generally excellent. Marks: 2/0. Comments: Gaultier, circa 1875. Value Points: very pretty tiny poupee is all original, wig signed 00, wearing Bourbonnais regional costume of France with red woolen gown trimmed with Alencon black lace, lace coiffe beneath woven chapeau named "A Deux Bonjours". $2200/2800

222. Superb Early French Bisque Bebe Jumeau with Original Wig and Comb

13" (33 cm.) Pressed bisque socket head, very large brown glass enamel inset eyes, painted lashes, feathered brows, accented nostrils and eye corners, closed mouth with pale accented lips, pierced ears, very pale lambswool wig over cork pate, French composition and wooden eight-loose-ball-jointed body with straight wrists. Condition: generally excellent. Marks: 8/0 (head) Jumeau Medaille d'Or Paris (body). Comments: Emile Jumeau, circa 1878. Value Points: splendid early bebe with entrancing expression, original wig with Jumeau comb, antique aqua silk dress may be original, muslin undergarments, brown leather shoes signed E. Jumeau Paris. $7500/9500

Cherries Jubilee

223. A Pretty All-Original French Bisque Bebe Jumeau
15" (38 cm.) Bisque socket head, deep blue glass paperweight inset eyes, painted lashes, rose blushed eye shadow, brush-stroked and feathered brows, accented nostrils and eye corners, closed mouth with shaded and accented lips, pierced ears, auburn mohair wig over cork pate, French composition and wooden fully-jointed body. Condition: generally excellent. Marks: Depose Tete Jumeau Bte SGDG 6 (head and artist check marks) Jumeau Medaille d'Or Paris (body). Comments: in unplayed with condition, the little bebe has original wig, pate, body, body finish, and wears original muslin chemise, red Jumeau socks, and Jumeau signed shoes. $4000/5500

224. French Doll's Wooden Bedroom Set
23"l. bed. The wooden bedroom set, of dark finished wood, comprises bed with carved headboard and bed posts, nice bed coverings; along with night stand and three drawer chest with metal hardware. Excellent for display with dolls about 15"-20". French, circa 1890. $400/500

225. French Candy Container as White Dog
7"h. Fur-covered paper mache dog posed in seated upright position has glass eyes, black nose, removable head for access to candy container torso. French, circa 1890. Very good condition. $300/400

226. Pair of Doll Bonnets with Decorative Berries
To fit bebe about 14"-16". The matched pair of bonnets is each elaborately woven straw with concave crest and decorated with interwoven maroon velvet ribbons and streamers, along with berries and leaves. Circa 1885. $400/500

227. Wonderful Petite French Bisque Bebe EJ, Size 1
9" (23 cm.) Pressed bisque socket head, large blue glass paperweight inset eyes, dark eyeliner, painted lashes, feathered brows, accented nostrils and eye corners, closed mouth with accented lips, pierced ears, auburn mohair wig over cork pate. French composition and wooden fully jointed body. Condition: generally excellent. Marks: Depose E. 1 J. (and artist checkmarks) Jumeau Medaille d'Or Paris (body). Comments: Emile Jumeau, circa 1884. Value Points: tiny size 1 bebe has beautiful expression, original wig, pate, body, body finish, muslin chemise, bebe corset, socks and white kidskin shoes. $6000/7500

228. French Doll's Bedroom Ensemble in Petite Size
10"l. bed. Of dark walnut-finish the ensemble features nicely carved bed with acorn finials, along with two matching side chairs with turned spindles, each upholstered in original red silk cushions or mattress with yellow tufting, the bed with pleated bolster pillow. Perfect for display with dolls 6"-10". Excellent condition. French, circa 1885, a rare size to find of doll furnishings. $700/900

229. Paper Mache and White Fur Kitten Candy Container
3"h. (8 cm.) A seated white kitten with hollow paper mache form covered with white fur features green glass eyes, pink nose, open mouth, long tail, stand-up ears, and a removable lid that allows access to candy container interior. Probably French, circa 1900, an unusual small size with delightful features. $300/400

Cherries Jubilee

230. 1930's Doll's Maple Armoire
19"h. (48 cm.) Of fine curly maple with cinnamon finish, the 1930's style armoire with three sections features a full-length oval mirror on the door of the center section with two side-flanking sections whose doors are decorated by elaborately carved medallions and border of matching carving above the doors. There is bronze trim around the center panel and as door pulls. Also included is a matching side chair. A beautifully constructed miniature furniture in seldom found style. Circa 1925. Excellent condition. $700/900

231. German Bisque Flapper Doll, 1369, by Cuno and Otto Dressel
14" (35 cm.) Bisque socket head with slender heart-shaped facial shape, blue glass sleep eyes, painted lashes, single stroke brows, accented nostrils and eye corners, closed mouth with center accent line, brunette human hair wig, composition and wooden ball-jointed adult female body with slender flapper style torso, elongated limbs, feet shaped for wearing high heels, nicely costumed . Condition: generally excellent. Marks: 1469 C&O Dressel Germany 2. Comments: Dressel, circa 1920. Value Points: rare model with lovely face and features, original body with original finish. $2000/2500

232. German Bisque Fashion Lady, "Gibson Girl" by Kestner
20" (51 cm.) Bisque shoulder head of adult woman with haughtily upturned oval face, slender elongated throat, blue glass sleep eyes, heavily lidded eyes with thick black eyeliner, brush-stroked brows, accented nostrils and eye corners, closed mouth with center accent line, brunette mohair wig in upswept fashion over plaster pate, kid body with slender style, pin-jointing, bisque forearms with elongated fingers, nicely costumed in Edwardian style silk frock, watch, undergarments, black net stockings, old brown leather heeled shoes. Condition: generally excellent. Marks: 172 7. Comments: "Gibson Girl", designed by the American illustrator Gibson as portrayal of society woman of the era, circa 1910, Kestner. Value Points: wonderful example of the portrait model by known artist, with great bisque, painting, original wig, pate, body. $2000/2500

233. German Bisque Portrait of Asian Woman, 1129, by Simon and Halbig
18" (46 cm.) Amber-brown tinted bisque socket head, brown glass sleep eyes in side-slanted sockets, black painted lashes, black highly arched brows,

accented nostrils and eye corners, open mouth, shaded and accented lips, four teeth, pierced ears, black mohair wig, amber tinted composition and wooden ball-jointed body, antique cotton kimono. Condition: generally excellent. Marks: SH 1129 dep 9. Comments: Simon and Halbig, circa 1895. Value Points: excellent detail of modeling with unusual complexion tone variation on the hard to find model. $1200/1800

234. German Bisque Portrait of Asian Child, 1329, by Simon and Halbig
18" (46 cm.) Amber tinted bisque socket head, small brown glass sleep eyes, painted lashes, black feathered brows, accented nostrils and eye corners, open mouth, accented lips, four porcelain teeth, pierced ears, black mohair wig, amber tinted composition and wooden ball-jointed body. Condition: generally excellent. Marks: Simon & Halbig Germany 1329 5. Comments: Simon and Halbig, circa 1900. Value Points: very lovely complexion with excellent bisque, original body and body finish. $1100/1300

235. German All-Bisque Portrait of Asian Child
7" (18 cm.) Lightly amber tinted bisque swivel head on matching bisque torso, brown glass eyes in side-slant eye sockets, black painted lashes and curvy brows, accented nostrils, closed mouth, black mohair wig, peg-jointed bisque arms and legs, painted white stockings and blue slippers with upturned toes, antique silk costume with embroidery. Condition: generally excellent. Comments: attributed to Simon and Halbig, circa 1890. Value Points: hard to find all-bisque model with uniquely designed bisque slippers. $800/1000

236. German Bisque Asian Lady, 1199, by Simon and Halbig
20" (51 cm.) Light amber tinted bisque socket head, brown glass sleep eyes in side-slant sockets, painted lashes, black brush-stroked brows, accented eye corners and nostrils, open mouth, accented lips, pierced ears, black mohair wig in upswept fashion, amber tinted composition and wooden ball-jointed body. Condition: generally excellent. Marks: SH 1199 Germany dep 8. Comments: Simon and Halbig, circa 1895. Value Points: rarer Asian model with superb detail of sculpting and fine dewy patina of bisque, original body and body finish, antique flowered silk kimono. $1600/1900

Cherries Jubilee

237. Beautiful French Bisque Bebe Bru, Size 2, with Original Bru Shoes

12" (31 cm.) Bisque swivel head on kid-edged bisque torso with modeled bosom and shoulder blades, brilliant blue glass paperweight inset eyes, dark eyeliner, painted lashes, slightly modeled brush-stroked brows, accented eye corners and nostrils, closed mouth with shaded and accented lips, hint of tongue tip, pierced ears, blonde mohair wig over cork pate, kid bebe body with Chevrot hinged hips, wooden lower legs, kid-over-wooden upper arms, bisque forearms. Condition: generally excellent. Marks: Bru Jne 2 (head and shoulder plate). Comments: Leon Casimir Bru, circa 1884. Value Points: superb petite bebe by the illustrious doll firm with captivating look, finest bisque and painting, original wig, pate, body, perfect bisque hands, antique costume, original leather shoes with silver buckles signed Bru Jne Paris. $11,000/15,000

238. French Wooden Framed Psyche Mirror

10"h. (25 cm.) An oval-arched mirror of walnut with inlay striping is arranged within a wooden bracket with carved detail, and able to be tilted forward and back. French, circa 1875. $400/500

239. Early French Sewing Presentation for Child

14" x 10" box. A wooden box with leather-like paper cover and elaborate bronze mounts and handles, hinges open to reveal interior fitted with a variety of sewing tools, glass-fronted boxes of colorful beads and pearls, little boxes with lithographed covers depicting children at play, containing more sewing supplies, threads, scissors, silver needle case, thimble, and more, including treasures stored in the pull-out drawer. French, circa 1885. Excellent condition. $500/700

240. French Bisque Poupee in Original Costume

15: (38 cm.) Bisque swivel head on kid-edged bisque shoulder plate, blue glass enamel inset eyes, painted lashes, feathered brows, accented nostrils and eye corners, closed mouth with center accent line, pierced ears, blonde mohair wig, kid gusset-jointed fashion body with shapely waist,

stitched and separated fingers. Condition: generally excellent. Marks: 2. Comments: attributed to Pierre-Francois Jumeau, circa 1875. Value Points: the delicately featured lady doll has lovely expression, very sturdy and clean original body, wears original silk grey plaid gown with magenta silk trim, leather boots with unusual maker's stamp, undergarments, and magenta velvet bonnet. $2500/3500

241. French Automaton "Marquise Riding a Donkey" by Vichy
13"l. 15"h. A bisque-headed lady with blue glass eyes, painted lashes, and brows, closed mouth, brunette curls, carton torso and legs posed to allow her to sit side-saddle on the donkey, wire upper arms, bisque forearms, is seated on a paper-mache donkey with flocked finish, glass eyes, elaborate head harness, and the entire arrangement is posed atop a three wheeled tinplate base that hides a mechanical device. When wound, the platform propels forward and in circles, while the lady's arms, holding the reins, move and down, she nods her head, and the donkey bobs its head up and down. Condition: slight frailty to original costume, mechanism functions well, hairline on forehead. Comments: attributed to Vichy, circa 1880. Value Points: rare and delightful automaton with amusing action, the lady with elaborate original costume. $3000/4000

242. Collection, Ten First Period Nancy Ann Storybook Dolls
each 5" (13 cm.) Each of ten dolls is of painted bisque with one-piece head and torso with head posed downward, painted upper glancing eyes with long lashes, bow-shaped mouth, mohair wig, loop-jointed arms and legs, painted white boots, black boots or flat black slippers. Condition: generally excellent, slight surface dust, girl with blue pants is missing legs, boy with rick-rack blouse has sparse hair and few paint flakes. Marks: America (back torso). Comments: the first period dolls from the Nancy Ann firm, made one year only in 1936. Value Points: extremely rare ensemble, each doll is wearing its original costume. $2500/3500

243. Collection, Nine Nancy Ann Storybook Dolls
each 5" (13 cm.) Each of nine dolls is of painted bisque with "O" shaped upper glancing eyes, bow-shaped mouth, painted flat black shoes. Five have jointed arms and legs including "I have a little pet" with white plush cat, Dainty Dolly, Little Betty Blue (wrist tag), "Mary at the Cottage Door" and girl in nylon taffeta dress with blue flowers; and four have straight legs including Goldilocks, Little Boy Blue, Mistress Mary, and The Snow Queen. Condition: generally excellent, no tags unless noted, all have boxes except one. Marks: Story Book Dolls. Comments: Nancy Ann, circa 1945. Value Points: included are some rare models, all in fine unplayed with condition. $400/500

244. Nancy Ann Storybook Wedding Party
4 1/4" – 6". Each of five dolls is of painted bisque with upper glancing eyes, dot-shaped mouth, jointed arms, straight legs, included are Bride with silver wrist tag and original box, Groom with gold wrist tag and original box, Bridesmaid with lavender tulle gown and bonnet, wrist tag; Ringbearer with painted white boots and wrist tag, and Flower Girl with painted white boots and wrist tag. Condition: generally excellent. Marks: Storybook Dolls USA. Comments: Nancy Ann Storybook Dolls, circa 1945. Value Points: beautiful ensemble wedding party in fine original condition. $400/500

245. Twelve Nancy Ann Storybook Dolls
4 1/2" – 5 1/2". Each is of painted bisque with upper glancing eyes. Three have jointed legs including Baby, October Girl with wrist tag, and Easter Parade with wrist tag; and nine with straight legs and original tags: December Girl, Tuesday's Child, Queen of Hearts, Friday's Child, April Girl, August Girl, Maytime, Flower Girl (no tag) and Wednesday's Child. Condition: generally excellent. Marks: Storybook Dolls USA. Comments: Nancy Ann Storybook Dolls, circa 1945. Value Points: in fine fresh condition, each with original box. $400/500

Cherries Jubilee

246. Collection, Eighteen English "Old Cottage" Dolls in Original Boxes each about 8". Each has head with painted features, wig, cloth body with armature shape, and is wearing its original costume. Included in the group are: Bustle Girl in Party Dress, Bride, Bustle Doll, Scottish Boy, Goose Girl, Elizabethan Nurse and Baby, Victorian Doll with Hoop, Stuart Lady, Dutch Girl, Pearly King, Dutch Boy, Elizabeth Boy, and Victorian Girl with Lace Bonnet (name of each stamped on the box except Bride). Each has original Old Cottage labels, and each is presented in its original box, some with original price tags from Frederick & Nelson department store in Seattle at $14.95. Also included are four others without original boxes. $500/800

247. German Vinyl Blonde-Haired Sasha by Gotz
16" (42 cm.) Vinyl socket head with light tan complexion, dark brown painted eyes, black upper eyeliner, white eye shadow, pale pink lips, rooted dark blonde hair, five piece body. Condition: generally excellent, uncostumed. Marks: Sasha Serie (head and torso). Comments: Gotz, under license from Sasha Morgenthaler, circa 1965, included (not shown) is red pinafore ensemble #217 from English Sasha era. Value Points: beautiful complexion with lovely painting of features. $900/1200

248. German Vinyl Red-Haired Sasha by Gotz
16" (42 cm.) Vinyl socket head with dark brown complexion, dark brown painted eyes, black upper eyeliner, white eye shadow, pale pink lips, rooted red hair, five piece body. Condition: generally excellent, uncostumed. Marks: Sasha Serie (head and torso). Comments: Gotz, under license from Sasha Morgenthaler, circa 1965. Value Points: beautiful color hair and facial complexion. $900/1200

249. Studio Portrait Girl, CI, by Sasha Morgenthaler
20" (50 cm.) Socket head and body of synthetic material with square-shaped face, full cheeks, brown painted eyes, black upper eyeliner with white shading, fringed lashes, tiny dot brows, long blonde human hair, jointing at shoulders and hips, cupped left hand. Condition: generally excellent. Marks: CI 21/155 (head) 21/155 (left foot) Sasha (dress tag). Comments: Sasha Morgenthaler, model CI, made in 1955. Value Points: superb example of the artist-made doll is wonderfully preserved, wearing her original tagged costume. $4000/5000

Cherries Jubilee

250. German Vinyl Blonde-Haired Sasha by Gotz
16" (42 cm.) Vinyl socket head with light complexion, dark blue painted eyes, black upper eyeliner, rose eye shadow, flat nose, closed mouth, coral lips, blonde rooted hair, five piece body. Condition: generally excellent. Marks: Sasha Serie (head and torso). Comments: Gotz, under license from Sasha Morgenthaler, circa 1965. Value Points: rarer model known as "no nose" wears original brown corduroy dress, matching panties, white pique pinafore, white socks and shoes. $1200/1500

251. German Vinyl Blonde-Haired Sasha by Gotz
16" (42 cm.) Vinyl socket head with light tan complexion, brown painted eyes, black upper eyeliner, pale blue eye shadow, flat nose, closed mouth, coral lips, blonde rooted hair, five piece body. Condition: generally excellent. Marks: Sasha Serie (head and torso). Comments: Gotz, under license from Sasha Morgenthaler, circa 1965. Value Points: rarer model known as "no nose" wears original brown corduroy dress with white collar, sandals. $1200/1500

252. Two Swiss Carved Wooden Dolls
8" and 13" (20 and 33 cm.) Each has carved wooden socket head with carved hair in elaborate braids around the head, painted facial features, blue or brown upper glancing eyes, dowel-jointed simplistically carved wooden body, jointing at shoulders, hips, elbows, and knees. Condition: generally excellent. Comments: Swiss, circa 1920. Value Points: elaborately carved hair in braided coronets, original costumes. $400/500

253. Swiss Carved Wooden Doll
13" (33 cm.) Carved wooden socket head with very dark carved hair in coronet braid around the head, painted dark brown eyes, black upper eyeliner, painted brows, closed mouth with hint of smile, blushed cheeks, all-wooden body with dowel-jointing at shoulders, elbows, hips, and knees. Condition: generally excellent. Comments: Swiss, circa 1920. Value Points: especially beautiful face with wonderfully carved hair and very detailed costume and bonnet. $500/700

254. Swiss Carved Wooden Doll with Alsatian Costume
7" (18 cm.) Carved wooden socket head with very dark carved hair in coronet braid around the head, painted brown upper glancing eyes, black upper eyeliner, painted brows, closed mouth, all-wooden body with dowel-jointing at shoulders, elbows, hips, and knees. Condition: generally excellent. Comments: Swiss, circa 1920. Value Points: especially beautiful face with wonderfully carved hair, wearing beautiful Alsatian costume. $400/500

255. American Wooden Doll, Model 110W, by Schoenhut
14" (36 cm.) Carved/pressed wooden socket head, brown sleep eyes, painted lashes, feathered brows, accented nostrils, open mouth, two upper teeth, blonde mohair wig over separate wooden cut pate, wooden spring-jointed body, nicely costumed in country style dress. Condition: generally excellent. Marks: Patented Sept. 13, 1926 (head stamp) Schoenhut Doll, Pat. Jan.17, '11 USA (body). Comments: Schoenhut, circa 1926, model 110W. Value Points: hard to find little toddler with fine original finish and complexion. $600/800

Cherries Jubilee

256. Four, American Wooden "Pinn Family" by Schoenhut
5" – 12" (13 cm.-31 cm.) Each is all wooden doll with bedpost style head and painted cartoon-like features, yarn hair, block torso, clothespin hands; several have original paper labels including Ty Pinn, Baby Pinn, Hattie Pin and Bobbie Pinn, and have Schoenhut stamp on foot. Also included is a family of three black dolls of similar construction and style in original costumes but unmarked. American, circa 1935. Excellent condition. $400/500

257. American Wooden Character, 312, by Schoenhut
14" (35 cm.) Carved/pressed wooden socket head, blue intaglio eyes with white eye dots, fringed brows, upturned nose, closed mouth with pensive expression, original blonde tacked-on wig, all-wooden spring-jointed body, antique costume includes dress, cap, leather shoes and original knit teddy. Condition: generally excellent. Marks: Schoenhut Doll Pat. Jan.17, 1911 USA. Comments: Schoenhut, circa 1915, model 312. Value Points: appealing wistful expression, original finish and wig. $700/900

258. American Wooden Character Girl, 312, by Schoenhut
14" (35 cm.) Carved/pressed wooden socket head, blue intaglio eyes with white eye dots, fringed brows, upturned nose, closed mouth with pensive expression,

original blonde tacked-on wig, all-wooden spring-jointed body, antique costume includes dress, cap, leather shoes and original knit teddy. Condition: generally excellent. Marks: Schoenhut Doll Pat. Jan.17, 1911 USA & Foreign Countries. Comments: Schoenhut, circa 1915, model 312. Value Points: very choice original finish retains fine lustrous finish, deeply intaglio eyes, original wig, antique costume. $900/1200

259. Cloth Character Doll in the Steiff Manner
16" (41 cm.) Felt swivel head with angular-shaped center-seamed face, side-angled eye sockets with tiny bead eyes, black curly brows, tiny painted mouth, stitched ears, black mohair wig in intricate applied style, muslin body, jointed limbs, felt hands and feet, wearing blue silk kimono with yellow sash and trim, sandals. Condition: very good. Comments: maker unknown, inspired by the

popular Steiff caricature dolls of 1920 era. Value Points: imaginative creation with good detail of construction on the unusual doll. $500/700

260. German Bisque Character "Baby Peggy" by Amberg
18" (46 cm.) Bisque socket head, small brown glass sleep eyes, painted curly lashes, short feathered brows, accented nostrils, closed mouth with prim smile, accent line between the lips, brunette human hair, composition and wooden ball-jointed body, antique costume. Condition: generally excellent. Marks: Germany 19c24 L.A. & S N>Y. 50 973/3. Comments: portrait doll of the child film star, Baby Peggy Montgomery, circa 1925. Value Points: very rare portrait of 1920's film star with appealing bisque and characterization. $2500/3000

261. German Mohair Teddy, Probably Steiff
16" (41 cm.) Champagne blonde mohair teddy with excelsior filling, swivel head, shoe button eyes, black embroidered nose and mouth, stitched ears, jointed arms and legs, felt paws, embroidered claws. Excellent condition, attributed to Steiff, circa 1925. $900/1200

262. Small German Golden Brown Mohair Teddy
10" (25 cm.) Golden brown mohair teddy with excelsior filling, swivel head, black shoe button eyes, brown embroidered nose, stitched ears, jointed elongated arms, hip-jointed legs, felt paws. Very good condition, few moth holes in felt. Germany, Steiff, circa 1915, an appealing size in beautiful color. $1200/1700

263. German Bisque Toddler, "Ox", by Schoneau and Hoffmeister
14" (36 cm.) Bisque socket head, blue glass sleep eyes, mohair lashes, painted lower lashes, short feathered brows, accented eye corners, open mouth, two porcelain teeth, tongue, brunette mohair wig, composition and wooden ball-jointed toddler body with side-hip jointing, wearing antique knit long-johns bonnet and white kidskin shoes with blue pom-poms. Condition: generally excellent. Marks: S pb (in star) H Ox Germany. Comments: Schoneau and Hoffmeister, circa 1915. Value Points: most appealing expression of awe enhanced by fine dewy patina, rarer toddler body. $900/1200

264. German Golden Mohair Teddy by Steiff
19" (48 cm.) Golden mohair teddy with excelsior filling, swivel head, shoe-button eyes, stitched ears, embroidered nose and mouth, jointed arms and legs, felt paws with stitched claws, original Steiff button in ear. Germany, circa 1925. Very good condition, few moth holes in paws, mohair sparse on nose. $900/1300

265. German Black Bisque Character Doll by Gebruder Kuhnlenz
16" (41 cm.) Black bisque socket head with tinted bisque, brown glass sleep eyes, black painted lashes and short feathered brows, accented nostrils, open mouth with richly shaded lips, two porcelain upper teeth, black fleeced wig.

brown composition and wooden fully jointed body with straight wrists, antique costume. Condition: generally excellent. Marks: 34.27. Comments: Gebruder Kuhnlenz. circa 1890. Value Points: outstanding characterization is enhanced by beautiful complexion. $1200/1500

266. Pair, German Bisque Miniature Dolls by Gebruder Kuhnlenz
7" (18 cm.) Each has black-complexioned bisque socket head, black glass inset eyes, accented eye corners and nostrils, open mouth, four teeth, black mohair wig, five piece paper mache black body with painted shoes. Condition: generally excellent. Marks: 34.17. Comments: Gebruder Kuhnlenz, circa 1895. Value Points: endearing little couple with excellent bisque, original bodies and costumes. $700/1000

267. Two, German All Bisque Dolls with Brown Complexions
each 4 1/2" (12 cm.) Includes light brown complexioned character doll with swivel head, highly characterized features, loop-jointed bisque arms and legs, bare feet, brown mohair wig, glass eyes, open mouth, marked 61-11, by Gebruder Kuhnlenz; and dark brown complexioned doll with one piece head and torso, brown glass eyes, closed mouth, loop-jointed limbs, bare feet, unmarked. Condition: generally excellent. Comments: one by Kuhnlenz, other by Kestner, circa 1895. Value Points: two rare little doll with appealing features. $600/900

268. German Black Bisque Character Doll
11" (28 cm.) Solid domed bisque socket head with rich brown complexion, dark brown glass inset eyes, painted lashes and brows, accented nostrils, closed mouth with coral lips, pierced ears, black fleeced wig, brown composition and wooden fully jointed body with straight wrists, antique costume. Condition: generally excellent. Comments: circa 1890, mystery maker. Value Points: petite little closed mouth doll with beautiful expression and bisque. $700/900

269. German Black Bisque Character Doll
13" (33 cm.) Solid domed bisque socket head with ebony-black complexion, dark brown glass inset eyes, painted lashes and brows, accented nostrils and eye corners, closed mouth with coral shaded lips, pierced ears, black composition and wooden fully-jointed body with straight wrists, nicely costumed. Condition: generally excellent. Comments: mystery maker, circa 1890. Value Points: beautiful petite doll with choice complexion and lips, original body and body finish. $900/1300

270. Beautiful Large German Bisque Child by Kammer and Reinhardt
31" (79 cm.) Bisque socket head, blue glass sleep eyes, mohair lashes, painted lashes, slightly brushstroked and feathered brows, accented nostrils and eye corners, open mouth, shaded and outlined lips, four porcelain teeth, pierced ears, blonde mohair wig, composition and wooden ball-jointed body, antique costume. Condition: generally excellent. Marks: K*R Simon & Halbig 80. Comments: Kammer and Reinhardt, circa 1910. Value Points: beautiful large child doll has original body and body finish, wig, gorgeous expression and bisque. $800/1100

271. Large German Bisque Child Doll with Extended Mohair Wig
31" (79 cm.) Bisque socket head, brown glass sleep eyes, painted lashes, slightly modeled brush-stroked and feathered brows, accented nostrils, open mouth with outlined lips, accented lips, four porcelain teeth, pierced ears, brunette mohair extended-length wig, composition and wooden ball-jointed body, antique costume. Condition: generally excellent, body one size small. Marks: Simon & halbig K*R 85. Comments: Kammer and Reinhardt, circa 1910. Value Points: beautiful matte bisque enhanced by rich decorative glaze on brows and lips, fabulous wig. $700/900

272. German Bisque Pouty, "Marie" by Kammer and Reinhardt
13 1/2" (34 cm.) Bisque socket head, blue painted downcast eyes, heavily modeled eyelids, black eyeliner, one stroke tapered brows, accented nostrils, closed mouth with accented lips, blonde mohair wig, composition and wooden ball-jointed body. Condition: generally excellent. Marks: K*R 101 34. Comments: Kammer and Reinhardt, circa 1912. Value Points: pretty character has original body, wig, well-defined features. $1800/3400

Cherries Jubilee

273. German All-Bisque Googly in Original Costume
5 1/2" (14 cm.) Solid domed bisque socket head, painted blue googly eyes glancing to the right, accented nostrils of pug nose, closed mouth with impish smile, blonde mohair wig, loop-jointed bisque arms and legs, painted blue bobby socks and black one-strap shoes, antique knit Tyrolean style costume. Condition: generally excellent. Comments: Germany, circa 1915. Value Points: endearing expression of the wide-eyed googly, excellent bisque. $500/700

274. German Bisque Toddler, 126, by Kammer and Reinhardt
10" (26 cm.) Bisque socket head, blue glass sleep eyes, mohair lashes, painted lashes, feathered brows, accented nostrils, open mouth, two porcelain teeth, brunette mohair bobbed wig, composition five piece toddler body with side-hip jointing. Condition: generally excellent. Marks: K*R Simon & Halbig Germany 126 23. Comments: Kammer and Reinhardt, circa 1920. Value Points: little toddler wears dainty pinafore, has original wig and body, body finish. $600/800

275. German Bisque Toddler, 126, by Kammer and Reinhardt
10" (26 cm.) Bisque socket head, brown glass sleep eyes, painted lashes, feathered brows, accented nostrils, open mouth, two porcelain teeth, brunette mohair bobbed wig, composition five piece toddler body with side-hip jointing. Condition: generally excellent, very faint hairline on forehead.

Marks: K*R Simon & Halbig 126 Germany 23. Comments: Kammer and Reinhardt, circa 1920. Value points: the little toddler has original wig, body, body finish, costume. $500/700

276. German Bisque "Mein Liebling" by Kammer and Reinhardt
27 1/2" (70 cm.) Bisque socket head, blue glass sleep eyes, dark eyeliner, painted lashes, short feathered brows, accented nostrils and eye corners, closed mouth with shaded and accented lips, blonde mohair wig, composition and wooden ball-jointed body, lovely antique costume. Condition: generally excellent. Marks: K*R Simon & Halbig 117 70. Comments: Kammer and Reinhardt, their model known as "Mein Liebling", circa 1912. Value Points: beautiful doll with gentle expression, loveliest bisque and decoration. $4500/6500

Cherries Jubilee

277. Pair, All Original German Bisque Toddlers by Herm Steiner
12" (31 cm.) Each has bisque socket head, blue or brown glass sleep eyes, painted lashes, short feathered brows, accented nostrils and eye corners, open mouth, two upper teeth, brunette mohair bobbed wig, composition five piece toddler body. Condition: generally excellent, shoes frail. Marks: HS (intertwined Germany. Comments: Herm Steiner, circa 1925. Value Points: In unplayed with condition, the pair of little toddlers are wearing their factory original toddler costumes. $900/1200

278. German Tinplate Toy Stove with Utensils
12"l. (31 cm.) Tinplate kitchen stove with three embossed oven doors, four burner holes with lidded pots on each including tea kettle and boiler, brass towel railing, claw feet, along with two miniature pot holders. Germany, probably Maerklin, circa 1900. $500/700

279. American Cloth Minnie Mouse Attributed to Charlotte Clark
15" (38 cm.) All cloth doll representing the comic character has white muslin mask face with embroidered black pie-cut eyes and lashes, black nose, thin line embroidered mouth, black cotton head and pleated rounded ears, black muslin body with stitched on yellow gloves of over-sized hands with four fingers, stitched-on red polka dotted heeled shoes, with matching collar, skirt and lace-edged pantalets. Condition: generally excellent. Comments: attributed to Charlotte Clark, early Disney designer, circa 1935. Value points: very rare figure with fine detail of construction, original costume. $1500/2500

280. German All-Bisque Miniature Doll "Vivi" by Orsini
5" (13 cm.) All-bisque head and torso, tiny brown glass eyes, painted lashes, feathered brows, accented nostrils, closed mouth with modeled space between the shaded and outlined lips, brunette mohair bobbed wig, loop-jointed bisque arms and legs, painted above-the-knee white ribbed stockings, black one-strap shoes, muslin chemise. Condition: generally excellent. Marks: JIO c. 1919 47 (incised) Vivi Reg.US Pat. Off. Corp 1920 J.I.Orsini. Pat. Appl'd For (paper label). Comments: designed by American artist Jeanne Orsini, circa 1920. Value Points: rare little all bisque with distinctive "pointing finger", original wig, paper label. $700/900

281. German Earthenware Character Baby Designed by Jeanne Orsini
14" circ (36 cm.) Solid domed earthenware head with flanged neck, dark brown glass sleep eyes, ochre eye

shadow, fringed brows, open mouth with smiling expression, two porcelain upper teeth, row of lower porcelain teeth, tongue, muslin body, composition arms and legs, antique costume. Condition: generally excellent. Marks: 7437/45 Germany. Comments: designed by American artist, Jeanne Orsini, circa 1925, made in Germany. Value Points: rare model with most distinctive expression. $400/600

282. German Bisque Farmer by Cuno and Otto Dressel
13" (33 cm.) Bisque socket head of older gentleman, brown glass inset eyes, brush stroked grey brows, incised age lines outlined in red, prominent nose, closed mouth with full smiling lips, white mohair wig and beard, composition and wooden fully-jointed body. Condition: generally excellent. Marks: S 1 Germany. Comments: Dressel, circa 1895, the model also appeared as Uncle Sam. Value Points: the Farmer wears his original striped cotton shirt, overalls, boots, felt hat and carries farm tools. $1200/1700

283. 19th Century Wooden Pull-toy Horse on Platform
18" (46 cm.) A wooden horse in prancing position has brown and white hide cover, horsehair mane and tail, brown glass eyes, carved open mouth and nostrils, and elaborate leather harness and saddlery, and is mounted upon a cast iron wheeled platform that is pencil-labeled 343/6 in script. Circa 1880. Excellent condition of the luxury toy. $1200/1500

Cherries Jubilee

284. French Brown Bisque Poupee by Gaultier
14" (36 cm.) Dark brown complexioned bisque swivel head on kid-edged bisque shoulder plate, dark brown glass inset eyes, painted lashes, closed mouth, pierced ears, black mohair wig over cork pate, brown kid fashion body with shapely waist and one piece shapely limbs, stitched and separated fingers. Condition: generally excellent. Marks: 1 (head) F.G. (shoulder plate). Comments: Gaultier, circa 1880. Value Points: rare brown-complexioned poupee wears lovely ivory silk fashion gown with extended train and trim, undergarments, straw bonnet. $3000/3500

285. Rare French Bisque Poupee by Denis-Duval
18" (46 cm.) Pale pressed bisque shoulder head with plump facial modeling, cobalt blue glass enamel inset eyes, painted lashes, feathered brows, accented nostrils, closed mouth

with center accent line, unpierced ears, blonde mohair wig over cork pate, French kid poupee body with gusset jointing, porcelain arms to above the elbows, shaped fingers. Condition: generally excellent. Marks: Brevete D.D. S.G.D.G. (green stamp on torso) Comments: Duval-Denis, circa 1861, the firm succeeded the Blampoix firm for two years only at this time. Value Points: very rare early signed poupee with beautiful expression, and wonderful antique folklore style costume including lace coiffe, wicker basket, undergarments, shoes. $4000/5000

286. German Bisque Doll with Glass Eyes and Sculpted Hair, with Miniature Doll

9" (23 cm.) Bisque shoulder head with blonde sculpted hair in short curls, cobalt blue glass enamel inset eyes, painted lashes, accented nostrils, closed mouth, old muslin body with bisque limbs, painted shoes, blue silk gown; along with smaller bisque baby with blonde sculpted hair, painted features, muslin body and bisque limbs, wearing brown velvet baby gown. Condition: generally excellent. Comments: Germany, circa 1870. Value Points: beautiful presentation of pair of dolls, the larger with rarer glass eyes. $800/1000

287. French Bisque Poupee Attributed to Blampoix with Trunk and Trousseau from A La Galerie de Vivienne

13" (33 cm.) Pink tinted porcelain shoulder head, painted cobalt blue eyes with dark upper eyeliner and painted lashes, feathered brows, accented nostrils and eye corners, closed mouth with center accent line, pale blonde mohair wig over cork pate, kid fashion body with gusset-jointed limbs, porcelain arms to above the elbows. Condition: generally excellent. Marks: Bte SGDG (front shoulder plate). Comments: attributed to Blampoix, circa 1860. Value Points: beautiful early painted eye poupee in petite size, antique costume and slippers, with trunk and trousseau of additional costumes, the trunk with original label of prestige doll boutique A La Galerie de Vivienne. $4500/6500

288. French Bisque Poupee by Jumeau

15" (38 cm.) Bisque swivel head on kid-edged bisque shoulder plate, blue glass enamel inset eyes, painted lashes, feathered brows, accented eye corners and nostrils, closed mouth with center accent line, pierced ears, blonde mohair wig over cork pate, French kid fashion body with gusset jointing, stitched and separated fingers, antique muslin chemise, red leather slippers signed "P". Condition: generally excellent, one patch of kid on right elbow. Marks: 5 (and artist checkmarks, on head) Jumeau Medaille d'Or Paris (body). Comments: Jumeau, circa 1880 Value Points: pretty poupee with rare signed body. $2000/2500

Cherries Jubilee

289. French Bisque Automaton "The Tricoteuse" by Roullet et Decamps
14" (36 cm.) A bisque-head doll with blue glass paperweight inset eyes, painted lashes and brows, open mouth, row of teeth, pierced ears, blonde mohair wig, carton torso and legs in seated position, wire upper arms, composition hands, is seated upon a maple wood chair, knitting held in her hands. When wound, the doll nods her head forward and back as though intently studying her handiwork, while her hands move back and forth as though knitting. Condition: generally excellent. Comments: Roullet et Decamps, circa 1900, the piece was listed in their catalogs as "Tricoteuse" (knitting lady). Value Points: amusing and well-preserved automaton with well-functioning movements. $5500/7500

290. Pair, German Bisque Figurines
each 12" (31 cm.) Each is one piece all bisque figure depicting a matched pair of man and woman in 18th century style country costumes, with woman holding a white dove and a white basket, the man with hand posed as though looking into the distance, a branch with a bird's nest of eggs held in his other hand. Maker's stamp on base. Excellent condition and beautifully detailed. Circa 1885. $500/700

291. French Pull-Toy Bulldog
22" (56 cm.) A firm-shaped bulldog with flocked finish has detailed musculature and realistic body posture and tiny hidden wheels in the feet, with hinged nodding head, large brown glass eyes, upright ears, hinged jaw with fierce sculpted teeth, original studded leather collar and ruff, pull-along chain that also causes his mouth to open and close in a ferocious manner, and the dog to bark. French, circa 1890. Excellent condition. $2000/2500

292. Very Grand French Bisque Bebe Jumeau, Size 16
33" (84 cm.) Bisque socket head, large blue glass paperweight inset eyes, dark eyeliner encircles the eye sockets, brush stroked and multi-feathered brows, accented eye corners, shaded nostrils, closed mouth with defined space between the shaded and outlined lips, separately modeled pierced ears, brunette human hair over cork pate, French composition and wooden fully-jointed body. Condition: generally excellent. Marks: Depose 16 (and artist checkmarks on head. Comments: Emile Jumeau, circa 1885. Value Points: rare grand size of Bebe Jumeau with gorgeous bisque having fine lustrous patina, original body and body finish. $12,000/15,000

293. Rare Bisque Swinging Doll for the French Market
10" (26 cm.) doll. Bisque shoulder head doll, with blue glass eyes, painted lashes and brows, open mouth, tiny teeth, blonde mohair wig, original firmly shaped body with wire upper arms and legs, composition lower legs with painted gold shoes, wooden hands, is wearing her original blue silk dress with lace trim, and matching cap, and holds a bentwood skipping hoop in her hand, the hoop decorated with red velour and blue ribbons. When the hoop is gently swung, the doll tumbles back and forth as though performing acrobatic tricks. Excellent condition. For the French market, circa 1895, very rare to find especially in this superb original condition. $900/1300

Cherries Jubilee

294. Early English Wooden Doll in Grand Size
24" (61 cm.) The wooden doll has egg-shaped head with elongated throat and torso with shapely front and flat back, black glass enamel inset eyes, tiny fringed lashes all around the eyes, fringed brows, shaped pointy tip nose, tiny closed mouth with painted lips, blushed cheeks, wig, simplistically carved dowel-jointed legs, cloth upper arms, muslin wrapped lower arms, wearing early homespun slip and pantalets, grey satin gown with metallic panels. Condition: generally excellent, few flaking spots but other wise finish is quite fine. Comments: England, circa 1780. Value Points: superb regal size of the early wooden doll with classic "dot" painted lashes and blushed rouge spots on cheeks. $12,000/16,000

295. Rare French Bisque Mystery Bebe
12" (31 cm.) Bisque socket head with ebony black complexion, unusual neck attachment with wooden bulb, brown glass paperweight inset eyes, painted black lashes and brows, accented nostrils, closed mouth with coral shaped lips, pierced ears, very lightweight French composition and wooden fully-jointed body with swivel wrists in original matching black complexion. Condition: generally excellent, tiny nose tip rub, body finish original albeit some crackling on torso. Marks: 3 (impressed on head). Comments: mystery maker, possibly Paris Bebe, circa 1890. Value Points: rare doll with beautiful face and eyes, original body, superb complexion. $3000/4000

296. Rare French Automaton "The Banjo Player" by Vichy
23" (58 cm.) Standing upon a green velvet covered base is a brown-complexioned man with paper mache head, highly characterized features, brown eyes with leather lashed lids, hinged jaw, elegantly shaped slender carton torso and legs, metal rod upper arms, composition forearms, wearing black tights, red silk jacket, ruffled shirt, sash, diamond fob, tall hat, and holding a wooden banjo. When wound, he moves his head in elaborate realistic movements, eyelids blink, mouth opens and closes as though he is singing in time to the tune he is strumming on his banjo. Condition: generally excellent, two fingers reglued. Comments: Vichy, circa 1880. Value Points: rare and well-preserved automaton, well-functioning with amusing manner, original finish, two tunes (original label on base). $8000/12,000

297. French Automaton "Chinese Opium Smoker" by Vichy
30" (76 cm.) Wax over paper mache headed Chinese man with leather-lidded brown glass eyes, highly characterized face, hinged jaw with black moustache, carton torso and legs, metal upper arms, paper mache hands with elegantly posed fingers, wearing antique (frail) silk robe with maroon sash and sleeves, black Chinese cap, and is holding an opium pipe in his right hand, and a cane in his left hand. A system of rubber tubing in his torso and right arm allows an impression that the figure is smoking when the mechanism is activated. When wound, he turns his head in an elaborate and realistic manner, while blinking his eye lids, and opening an closing his mouth as though inhaling, his arms alternately lift the pipe and cane. Condition: finish original albeit worn, mechanism functions albeit rubber tubing frail and unpredictable. Comments: Vichy, circa 1880. Value Points: rare early automaton with original accessories and regal posture. $8000/12,000

Cherries Jubilee

298. "Grand Jeu de Bebe Jumeau" from 1889 Paris Exposition
17" x 26", 26" x 35" framed. Game board from "Grand Jeu du Bebe Jumeau" created by Emile Jumeau as a publicity object for the 1889 Universal Exposition in Paris: the game featured the friendship between France and America, and praised the French doll in preference to the inferior German dolls (players lost points in the game when they landed on German doll spots). Excellent condition, framed and matted. 1889, few original posters are extant. $1000/1400

299. French Bisque Automaton "Girl with Tambourine and Bell" by Roullet et Decamps
18" overall (46 cm.) Standing upon a brocade covered wooden base is a bisque-headed doll with brown glass paperweight inset eyes, painted lashes and brows, accented nostrils and eye corners, closed mouth with accented lips, pierced ears, blonde mohair wig over cork pate, carton torso and legs, wire upper arms, bisque forearms, maroon silk and lace costume, holding a tambourine in right hand and bell in the other. When wound she moves her head side to side, nods, and alternately shakes the tambourine and then the bell, while music plays. Condition: generally excellent, mechanism and music function well. Marks: Depose Tete Jumeau Bte SGDG 1 (head). Comments: Roullet et Decamps, circa 1895. Value Points: pretty little girl with amusing action, dramatic large eyes. $4000/6000

300. French Bisque First Period Bebe EJ by Jumeau
20" (51 cm.) Pressed bisque socket head, brown glass paperweight inset eyes, painted lashes, feathered brows, mauve blushed eye shadow, accented eye corners, shaded nostrils, closed mouth with defined space between the shaded and outlined lips, separately modeled and pierced ears, brunette human hair wig over cork pate, French composition and wooden eight-loose-ball-jointed body with straight wrists. Condition: generally excellent. Marks: 7 EJ (head) Jumeau Medaille d'Or Paris (body). Comments: Jumeau, circa 1882, the first

period of the EJ model. Value Points: beautiful bebe with well detailed sculpting, full cheeks with delicate blush, original body and body finish, choice bisque, lovely antique maroon velvet and silk costume, lace bonnet, signed Jumeau shoes. $6500/8500

301. French Doll-Sized Wooden Gilt Piano with Music Box
22"l (56 cm.). A wooden ballroom piano is richly finished in gold leaf with hand-painted designs of frolicking cherubs and Fragonard style paintings. The piano was designed for a child's play with working keyboard, and hinged compartment that contains a xylophone (wooden mallet included), and also has keywind music box that functions well. The hinged lid reveals a large hollow compartment at the back that indicates the piano was originally presented as a candy box, later to be used for play purposes. A rare and superbly preserved and painted accessory, perfect for doll display. $1200/1800

302. French Bisque Bebe Jumeau, Size 9
20" (51 cm.) Bisque socket head, blue glass paperweight inset eyes, dark painted lashes, painted brows with decorative glaze, accented nostrils and eye corners, closed mouth with shaded and outlined lips, pierced ears, brunette human hair over cork pate. French composition and wooden fully-jointed body. Condition: generally excellent. Marks: Depose Tete Jumeau 9 (head) Bebe Jumeau Bte SGDG Depose (body). Comments: Emile Jumeau, circa 1890. Value Points: very beautiful bebe with rich painting, original wig, body, body finish, antique gold silk twill costume may be original, lovely undergarments, fancy straw and silk bonnet, signed Jumeau shoes. $3500/4500

302A. French Bisque Bebe Jumeau, Incised Depose Mark, with Original Costume
14" (36 cm.) Bisque socket head, blue glass paperweight inset eyes in deeply set eye sockets, painted lashes, brush stroked brows, accented nostrils and eye corners, closed mouth, accented lips, pierced ears, brunette human hair over cork pate. French composition and wooden fully jointed body with straight wrists. Condition: generally excellent. Marks: Depose Jumeau 5 (incised on head) Jumeau Medaille d'Or Paris (body). Comments: Emile Jumeau, circa 1885. Value Points: pretty bebe with rarely found signature, made for one year only, wears her original Jumeau couturier dress, leather shoes signed Bebe Jumeau Depose 5. $4500/6500

303. Grand French Porcelain Poupee with Enamel Eyes Attributed to Blampoix
25" (64 cm.) Pink-tinted porcelain shoulder head with plump rounded face, cobalt blue glass enamel inset eyes, dark eyeliner, painted lashes, feathered brows, accented eye corners and nostrils, closed mouth with center accent line, unpierced ears, auburn mohair wig over cork pate. French kid gusset jointed body with stitched and separated fingers and toes, antique calico dress, undergarments, straw bonnet, shoes. Condition: generally excellent. Comments: attributed to Blampoix, circa 1860. Value Points: beautiful large early poupee with fine lustrous patina of complexion, brilliant eyes, original body. $4500/5500

304. French Maitrise Model Walnut Desk
9"l. (23 cm.) Fine cabinetmaker's quality miniature desk, known as "maitrise model", is of rich walnut with roll front of burled wood outlined with a double strip of inlays, the front opens to reveal leather tooled writing surface and pen tray, one full-length tray. Excellent condition of the elegantly shaped furniture with beautiful woods. French, early 19th century. $900/1300

305. French Stenciled Miniature Desk
8" (20 cm.) Wooden desk with mahogany finish has two bottom drawers, fancy spindled sides, S-shaped desk front, beaded trim, fancy crest, and is decorated with elaborately stenciled scrolls in gold leaf enclosed red and blue colors. French, circa 1880. Excellent condition. $500/700

306. French Bisque Poupee with Elaborate Head Articulation
22" (56 cm.) Pale bisque swivel head on kid-edged shoulder plate. articulation allowing the head to tilt forward. and from side to side based on the Dehors deposed system. pale blue/grey enamel eyes with spiral threading and darker blue outer rims, painted lashes. feathered brows, accented eye corners and nostrils, very delicate mauve eyeshadow, closed mouth with accented and shaded lips. pierced ears. French bisque body with gusset-jointed hips and knees.
bisque forearms. lovely maroon silk gown. bonnet. undergarments. unusual green velvet heeled shoes. Condition: generally excellent, bisque forearms are not original. Marks: 7 (front shoulderplate). Comments: circa 1867. maker unknown. Value Points: beautiful poupee with exquisite decoration. $2500/3500

307. French Bisque Poupee by Blampoix
21" (53 cm.) Pale bisque swivel head on kid-edged bisque shoulder plate. cobalt blue glass inset eyes. thick black eyeliner. painted lashes. feathered brows. accented eye corners and nostrils, closed mouth with center accent line, pierced ears, blonde mohair wig over cork pate. French kid fashion body with shapely torso and gusset-jointing. green silk gown. Condition: generally excellent. body dusty but very firm. Marks: 6 (head and shoulders). Comments: attributed to Blampoix, circa 1860. Value Points: fine large size with beautiful pale bisque contrasting the brilliant cobalt blue eyes. $3000/3500

308. French Bisque Premiere Bebe by Jumeau
15" (38 cm.) Pressed bisque socket head. large brown glass enamel inset eyes. painted lashes. mauve blushed eye shadow. arched feathered brows. accented eye corners and nostrils. closed mouth with outlined pale lips, pierced ears. blonde mohair wig over cork pate. French composition and wooden eight loose-ball-jointed body with straight wrists. antique costume. undergarments. socks. leather shoes signed M.G. Condition: generally excellent. Marks: 6 (head) Jumeau Medaille d'Or Paris (body). Comments: Emile Jumeau. circa 1878. Value Points: the first model bebe by Jumeau with very lovely bisque enhanced by fine painting. original wig. body. body finish. $5500/7500

Cherries Jubilee

309. Grand French Bisque Bebe by Denamur, Size 14
31" (79 cm.) Bisque socket head, large blue glass paperweight inset eyes, thick black eyeliner, painted lashes, rose blushed eye shadow, widely arched brush stroked brows with feathered highlights, accented eye corners and nostrils, closed mouth with shaded and accented lips, pierced ears, blonde mohair wig over cork pate, French composition and wooden fully-jointed body, lovely antique costume. Condition: generally excellent. Marks: E. 14 D. Depose. Comments: Denamur, circa 1890. Value Points: unusually large size of the pretty bebe with dramatic large eyes, fine bisque. $3000/4000

310. French Armoire with Contents and Bisque Doll
21" (53 cm.) armoire, 11" (28 cm.) doll. Wooden armoire with fancy crest, mirrored front door that opens to reveal a bisque-head doll with glass eyes, open mouth, blonde mohair wig, five piece French composition body, wearing original chemise; on the other side of the armoire is a glass front cabinet with three shelves of neatly tied house linens, and three drawers with tied-in accessories including brush, soap, powder puff and others, and long bottom drawer as sewing necessaire with scissors, thimble, thread, and such. Excellent condition. French, circa 1895, a presentation armoire from French department store Etrennes catalogs, and rare to find in this condition. $1800/2500

311. French Bisque Bebe Steiner
14" (36 cm.) Bisque socket head, blue glass paperweight inset eyes, painted lashes, thick brush stroked brows, accented nostrils and eye corners, closed mouth, accented lips, pierced ears, blonde mohair wig over Steiner pate, Steiner composition and wooden fully-jointed body. Condition: generally excellent. Marks: A-7 (head) Le Petit Parisien Bebe Steiner (body label). Comments: Jules Steiner, circa 1890. Value Points: pretty little bebe with lovely bisque, original body and body finish, silk costume, antique shoes and socks. $2800/3500

312. French Bisque Paris Bebe by Danel et Cie
19" (48 cm.) Bisque socket head, large brown glass paperweight inset eyes, dark eyeliner, painted lashes, brushstroked brows, accented nostrils, closed mouth with defined space between the lips, brunette human hair over cork pate, French composition and wooden fully-jointed body. Condition: generally excellent. Marks: Paris Bebe Tete Dep 8 (head) Paris Bebe Depose (and Eiffel Tower symbol, on body). $3000/3500

313. German Bisque Figurine by Gebruder Heubach
16" (41 cm.) One piece all-bisque figure of young girl with light brown curly hair in dancing pose, with pointing toe, arms held gracefully to the side holding up the pleats of her skirt, on self base against a bower of roses; with deeply intaglio sculpted eyes, painted features, richly sculpted costume, with Heubach sunburst symbol on back. A rare size with beautiful details. Germany, Heubach, circa 1900. $1200/1500

314. French Bisque Bebe by Rabery and Delphieu
21" (53 cm.) Bisque socket head, brown glass paperweight inset eyes, painted lashes, widely arched brows, accented eye corners and nostrils, closed mouth with pale accented lips, pierced ears, brunette mohair wig over cork pate, French composition and wooden fully-jointed body with straight wrists, antique costume. Condition: generally excellent. Marks: R. 2 D. Comments: Rabery and Delphieu, circa 1888. Value Points: pretty girl with deeply impressed dimples at lip corners and above the upper lip, fine quality of bisque, original body and body finish. $3000/4000

Cherries Jubilee

Cherries Jubilee

315. Petite German Bisque Closed Mouth Child by Kestner
11" (28 cm.) Bisque socket head, brown glass sleep eyes, painted lashes, brush stroked and feathered brows, accented nostrils and eye corners, closed mouth with center accent line, blonde mohair wig over plaster pate, composition and wooden ball-jointed body, antique undergarments, bracelet, leather shoes and socks. Condition: generally excellent. Marks: made in Germany 128. Comments: Kestner, circa 1890. Value Points: pristine condition of the very pretty petite child with original wig, pate, body, body finish, closed mouth. $1200/1800

316. German Bisque Bye-Lo in Original Box
13" circ. head (33 cm.) Solid domed bisque socket head with lightly tinted baby hair and brows, blue glass sleep eyes, painted lashes, accented nostrils, closed mouth with center accent line, muslin frog-shaped body especially designed for this doll by the artist, celluloid hands. Condition: generally excellent. Marks: copr. by Grace S. Putnam, made in Germany (head) (body also stamped). Comments: Bye-lo Baby, designed by American artist Grace S. Putnam, 1923. Value Points: the infant baby wears elaborate gown and undergarments, and is preserved in its original box labeled "Bye-lo Baby, The Almost Human Doll, George Borgfeldt, New York". $600/800

317. German Dollhouse Furnishings and Doll in Original Box
10" x 10" box. 3" doll. A cardboard box with decorative papers and lithograph design has perfectly preserved interior, comprising parlor furniture of patterned green velvet with fringed skirt (sofa, two arm chairs, four side chairs, stool), white marble round pedestal table, mantel clock, along with an all-bisque doll with sculpted bobbed hair, original costume. Excellent condition throughout. Germany, circa 1910. Rare to find furniture style, the value enhanced by original presentation. $700/1000

318. Pair, German All Bisque Miniature Dolls in Original Costumes
3" (8 cm.) Each is all-bisque with one piece head and torso, painted facial features, brown bobbed mohair wig, pin-jointed limbs, brown painted shoes. Condition: generally excellent. Comments: Germany, circa 1910. Value Points: the little boy and girl wear factory original matching red felt suits and caps, each with tiny belt. $400/600

319. German Bisque Googly by Goebel
7" (18 cm.) Solid domed bisque socket head, painted orange hair with forelock curl and blue headband and bow, painted facial features, side-glancing googly eyes, painted upper lashes, dot brows, closed mouth with impish smile, five piece paper mache body, painted stockings and blue shoes. Condition: generally excellent. Marks: (crown symbol) P 12/0. Comments: Goebel, circa 1925. Value Points: most appealing little googly with fine enhancing glaze on hair and ribbon. $400/500

320. Two Italian Cloth Dolls by Lenci
Including a 9" (23 cm.) smaller doll with felt swivel head, painted features, side-glancing wide open eyes, "O" shaped mouth, brunette wig, five piece body, wearing original felt costume of the Italian youth

army with brass-buttoned green felt uniform and elaborately feathered cap, original Lenci paper label; along with felt hand puppet of Spanish troubadour with vivid red and orange felt costume, black hat with dangling rose and carrying wooden sword. Condition: both exceptionally fresh and colorful. Comments: Lenci, circa 1935. Value Points: rare models to find in wonderfully preserved condition. $1200/1500

Cherries Jubilee

321. Pair, American Black Cloth Folk Dolls in Original Costumes
12" (31 cm.) Each is of black stockinette with flat-dimensional faces except sewn-on flat nose patch, embroidered eyes and pupils, brows, and red lips, black yarn fleecy hair on man, woman with bald head under stitched on cap, all black stockinette bodies. Condition: generally excellent. Comments: folk art American dolls, circa 1900. Value Points: well preserved little pair with imaginative construction, original costumes. $700/900

322. Group, American Wooden Characters by Schoenhut
8" Barney. Each is all-wooden with painted and sculpted hair and facial features, including Barney Google (with original paper label), Spark Plug, Max and Moritz and Baby Danny Doodles. Each fair condition, costumes original although possibly Spark Plug blanket replaced. Circa 1915. $900/1100

323. American Wooden Girl by Schoenhut, Model 107
11" (28 cm.) Carved/pressed wooden socket head, small painted blue eyes, black upper eyeliner, tinted brows, accented nostrils of rounded pug nose, closed mouth with pouty expression, blonde mohair tacked-on wig, wooden spring-jointed body with toddler legs, antique costume and shoes. Condition: generally excellent. Marks: HE Schoenhut c. 1913. (head) Schoenhut Doll, Pat. Jan.17.'11 USA. Comments: Schoenhut, circa 1914, model 107. Value Points: the character expression is enhanced by very plump cheeks, original finish and patina, original wig, antique dress. $600/800

324. American Wooden Boy by Schoenhut, Model 107
11" (28 cm.) Carved/pressed wooden socket head, small painted blue eyes, black upper eyeliner, tinted brows, accented nostrils of rounded pug nose, closed mouth with pouty expression, brunette mohair tacked-on wig, wooden spring-jointed body with toddler legs, antique costume and shoes. Condition: generally excellent. Marks: Schoenhut Doll. Pat. Jan.17.'11 USA and Foreign Countries. Comments: Schoenhut, circa 1917, model 107. Value Points: dear little doll in wonderful size has original wig, original painting with fine patina. $600/800

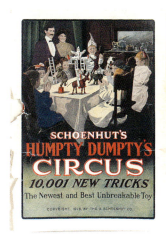

325. Original Schoenhut Catalog, 1918
7" x 10". A 46 page catalog is filled with circus figures showing them in various performing positions, plus all the accessories available, other circus-sized figures such as Mary and Farmer, and four pages of dolls. Binding weak, cover loose. A rare and informative catalog. $300/500

326. American Wooden Boy by Schoenhut, Model 107, with Painted Hair
11" (28 cm.) Carved/pressed wooden socket head, small painted dark blue eyes, black upper eyeliner, tinted brows, accented nostrils of rounded pug nose, closed mouth with pouty expression, solid pate with tinted tan hair, wooden spring-jointed body with toddler legs, antique costume and shoes. Condition: generally excellent. Marks: Schoenhut Doll. Pat. Jan.17.'11 USA and Foreign Countries. Comments: Schoenhut, circa 1917, model 107. Value Points: fine original lustrous finish on the pouty toddler with painted hair. $500/700

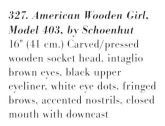

327. American Wooden Girl, Model 403, by Schoenhut
16" (41 cm.) Carved/pressed wooden socket head, intaglio brown eyes, black upper eyeliner, white eye dots, fringed brows, accented nostrils, closed mouth with downcast

expression, blonde mohair tacked on wig, all wooden spring-jointed body. Condition: fine professional restoration for perfect original look. Marks: Schoenhut Doll. Pat. Jan.17.'11 USA and Foreign Countries. Comments: Schoenhut, circa 1914, model 403. Value Points: beautiful doll wears antique cotton dress that may be original, original knit teddy and Schoenhut stockings, Schoenhut shoes, white pique sun hat. $700/900

328. American Wooden Character Girl, Model 328, by Schoenhut
18" (46 cm.) Carved/pressed wooden socket head, deeply intaglio brown eyes, black upper eyeliner, prominent white eye dots, fringed brows, accented nostrils, closed mouth with downcast expression, blonde mohair wig, all wooden spring-jointed body. Condition: fine professional restoration, perfect original look. Marks: Schoenhut Doll. Pat. Jan.17.'11 USA and Foreign Countries. Comments: Schoenhut, circa 1914, model 328. Value Points: beautiful doll wears antique pink cotton dress that may be original, has superb carving. $700/900

329. Set, American Humpty Dumpty Circus by Schoenhut in Reduced Size
6 1/2" ringmaster. Each is all-wooden carved figure depicting various persons and animals of the circus, in reduced size, including Ringmaster, Lady rider, clown, donkey, deer with painted eyes and original leather antlers and ears, deer with glass eyes and original antlers and ears, gazelle with glass eyes and original leather horns and ears, one chair, one ladder, three barrels and barbells. Good to very good finish, some paint play wear but all original finishes, ringmaster missing hat, other costume elements originals. Schoenhut, circa 1925. $1100/1800

Cherries Jubilee

330. English Cloth Doll by Norah Wellings
21" (53 cm.) All cloth doll with swivel head, pressed and painted facial features, brown side-glancing eyes, painted lashes, fringed brows, accented nostrils, closed mouth, brunette braids, elongated torso and limbs. Condition: generally excellent. Comments: Norah Wellings, circa 1930. Value Points: in pristine condition, the doll wears vivid costume of yellow and green velvet with felt appliqué flowers, matching bonnet, stitched on black velvet shoes, and is preserved in her original labeled box. $700/900

332. Large American Composition Dionne Doll by Alexander
20" (51 cm.) All composition doll has socket head, brown sleep eyes, real lashes, painted lashes, arched brows, accented eye corners and nostrils, open mouth, four teeth, brunette human hair, composition five piece toddler body, wearing original pink dress, muslin slip and panties, pink lightweight woolen coat with self-covered buttons, black velvet collar, matching cap, shoes and socks. Condition: generally excellent. Marks: Alexander (doll) (dress and coat also tagged). Comments: Alexander, circa 1935. Value Points: wonderful large size of the Dionne doll with original tagged costume, booklet. $600/900

333. Set, American Composition Dionne Quintuplets by Alexander
each 8" (20 cm.) Each is all composition, with socket head, painted facial features, brown eyes, painted lashes and brows, rosebud-shaped mouth, brunette mohair wig, five piece composition body, wearing original pastel pique romper suit and bonnet (one bonnet missing). Condition: generally excellent, slight dust to costume. Marks: Alexander (dolls) (costumes also tagged Alexander). Comments: complete set of Dionne Quintuplets, Alexander, circa 1935. Value Points: appealing set with original wigs, costumes, shoes and pins. $900/1300

334. American Composition Doll by Madame Alexander
14" (36 cm.) Composition socket head, brown sleep eyes, real lashes, painted lower lashes, feathered brows, "O" shaped mouth, brunette mohair wig, five piece composition body, wearing original yellow

nylon floor-length gown with sheer overlay, ribbons, reticule, panties, shoes. Condition: generally excellent. Marks: Mme Alexander (doll) Madame Alexander New York USA. Comments: Alexander, circa 1935. Value Points: beautiful doll with fine original condition, lovely original tagged costume. $500/700

335. Set, American Composition Storybook Dolls, "Little Red Riding Hood"
each 10" (25 cm.) Each is all-composition with socket head depicting character from the fairy tale, viz. wolf, grandmother and little Red Riding Hood girl, with distinctive facial features, five piece composition body. Condition: generally excellent. Comments: circa 1935, the dolls are contained, unmarked, in the lid of their original display box. Value Points: rare set in fine unplayed with condition, each doll wearing its original fresh costume. $600/900

336. American Composition Doll "Jane Withers" by Alexander
13" (33 cm.). Composition socket head, dark sleep eyes, real lashes, painted lower lashes, arched brows, closed mouth with center accent line, brunette mohair wig, five piece composition body, wearing original flowered cotton dress, muslin chemise and panties, shoes, socks, pink hat. Condition: generally excellent, slight surface dust. Marks: Jane Withers All Rights Reserved Madame Alexander, NY (costume tag). Comments: Alexander, circa 1935. Value Points: rare doll with all original costume. $800/1100

Cherries Jubilee

337. American Composition Doll with Molly-E Outfit
18" (46 cm.) Composition socket head on composition shoulder plate, green sleep eyes, mohair lashes, painted lashes, open mouth, row of teeth, brunette mohair wig, muslin torso, composition arms and legs. Condition: generally excellent. Comments: Shirley Temple look-a-like, circa 1935. Value Points: the little doll wears an original Molly-E outfit comprising plaid jacket and cap, matching umbrella, boots, orange polka dot romper suit. $400/500

338. Composition "Ella Cinders" by Horsman
18" (46 cm.) Composition head with painted blue side-glancing eyes, freckles, rosy cheeks, black mohair bobbed wig, muslin torso, composition limbs, wearing original red and white checkered dress with apron, bloomers, socks, shoes. The doll is marked c. M.N.S. and the costume is tagged "Horsman Doll, Made in USA". Horsman, circa 1925, the model is rarely found in this wigged version. Excellent condition except split on side of right leg. $800/1100

339. Composition "Betty Boop" by Cameo
12" (30 cm.) Composition over-sized socket head with black hair in tight spit curls in classic Betty Boop style, large googly side-glancing eyes, painted upper lashes, curvy brows, button-shaped nose, bow-shaped tiny mouth, composition torso, wooden segmented arms, composition legs, original dress and shoes. Good condition, original finish, surface craze lines on hair and face. Circa 1930. $700/900

Cherries Jubilee

340. Composition "Puzzy" in Original Costume
16" (41 cm.) Over-sized composition head with sculpted red hair, large side-glancing "O" shaped eyes, freckles, chubby cheeks, five piece composition body, wearing original one piece suit with white shirt and black slacks, red tie, shoes, socks. Marked "H of P USA". Designed by Herman Cohen of the House of Puzzy, circa 1948. Excellent condition. $400/500

341. Composition Advertising "Hotpoint" Doll by Cameo
15" (38 cm.) Over-sized composition socket head with H symbol on crown, side-glancing googly eyes, wide smile, composition torso with chubby tummy, all wood-segmented body with slits cut in hands for holding of promotional pieces. Original paper label "Art Quality Dolls, Cameo Products, Port Alleghany, Des & c. by JLK. Designed by Joseph Kallus for Hotpoint Appliances, circa 1930. Good condition, torso crazed. $700/900

342. Composition Advertising "General Electric Radio" Doll by Cameo
18" (46 cm.) Composition head portraying brightly smiling man, with wooden tall parade hat, composition torso with red sculpted marching uniform jacket, labeled GE with inset yellow rope trim, wooden segmented arms and legs, slits in hands for holding promotional pieces. Original paper label "Art Quality Dolls, Cameo Products, Port Alleghany, Des & c. by JLK." Designed by Joseph Kallus for Hotpoint Appliances, circa 1930. Very good condition, some facial wear. $700/900

343. Composition Advertising "RCA Radiotron" Doll by Cameo
16" (41 cm.) Composition head portraying page with pageboy hair, under large wooden hat in the shape of a radio tube, composition torso with sculpted shirt and banner RCA Radiotrons, all-wooden body with segmented limbs, slits in hands for holding of promotional pieces, original vivid painting. Original paper label "Art Quality Cameo Dolls". Designed by Joseph Kallus for RCA as a promotional figure, circa 1930. Excellent condition, few flakes on one collar point. $700/900

344. Composition "Superman" by Ideal
13" (33 cm.) Composition head with sculpted hair and classic Superman visage, on composition torso with sculpted hero's muscled chest, all wood segmented lower torso and limbs, original blue, yellow and red paint with Superman emblem on chest, (cape not original). Marked "Des. & Copyright by Superman Inc. Made by Ideal Novelty & Toy". Excellent condition. Circa 1940. $800/1200

Cherries Jubilee

345. Composition "Jeep" by Cameo
13" (33 cm.) Composition over-sized ball-shaped head with stuck-out pink-lined ears, long red nose, black ball-shaped eyes, five piece composition body with amusing shape, wood-segmented tail, blue spots on back torso. Marked "Jeep c. 1935 King Features Syn." Cameo, circa 1935. $800/1100

346. Composition "Pete" by Cameo
11" (28 cm.) Composition over-sized head with puppy ears, large googly side-glancing eyes, red ball nose, wide smile, dimples, all-wooden segmented body with green shirt, yellow gloves, black pants, orange shoes. Marked "Pete, Des. & Copyright by J.L. Kallus". Cameo, circa 1937. Excellent condition, slight wear at back of head. $700/900

347. Composition "King Little" by Ideal
13" (33 cm.) Composition head with sculpted grey hair, "O" shaped googly side-glancing eyes, painted moustache, wooden crown, composition torso with painted tunic and jacket, wooden segmented lower torso and limbs. In original vivid colors of grey, red, yellow and brown. Marked "King Little, c. by Paramount Pictures, Inc 1939, Made by Ideal Novelty and Toy". Excellent condition, few small paint rubs. $800/1000

348. Composition "Gabby" by Ideal
10" (26 cm.) Composition over-sized head with brown sculpted hair, very thick bushy brows, bulbous nose, scowl, composition torso with yellow shirt and brown collar, all wooden lower torso and segmented limbs in green and yellow colors, brown wooden feet. Marked "Gabby by Paramount Pictures Inc, Made by Ideal Novelty and Toy Co". Ideal, circa 1939. Good condition, original finish, some wear. $400/500

349. Composition "Howdy Doody" with Original Label
13" (33 cm.) Composition socket head with classic features of the TV star, red hair, freckles, all wooden body with swivel waist, wood-segmented body in various colors. Marked "Howdy Doody c. Bob Smith", on front chest paper label. Very good condition, original finish. $600/900

350. "Jiminy Cricket" Composition Doll
10" (25 cm.) Composition egg-shaped socket head in original cricket green color, "O" shaped side-glancing eyes, smiling expression, composition bug body and over-sized feet, jointed composition arms and yellow four-finger hands, original cloth jacket and hat. Marked "Jiminy Cricket W.D. Prod N&T Co. USA". Circa 1938. Excellent condition, hat faded, one foot reglued. $500/700

351. "Kayo" Composition Doll
13" (33 cm.) Composition socket head with modeled typical derby hat and brown hair, side-glancing googly eyes, hinged jaw that opens and closed from pull-string at back of head, one piece body with painted costume and pants, with original label "Kayo by Willard. Licensed by F.A.S". Very good condition, splits at each corner of mouth. Circa 1925. $200/300

Cherries Jubilee

352. Composition "Popeye" by Cameo
12" (31 cm.) Composition socket head with protruding jaw and bulbous nose, squinting eyes, pipe in mouth, modeled cap, composition torso with swivel waist, elongated chest, wooden segmented arms and legs with muscles, painted blue legs, orange shoes. Marked "Popeye c. 1935 King Features syn." Good condition, chest repainted, some wear to head. $300/400

353. Composition "Ferdinand the Bull"
10"l. (26 cm.) Composition head with large dreamy eyes, painted lashes, horns, on composition torso, four jointed legs, rope tail. Marked "Ferdinand the Bull" (white stencil) and C. W.D. Ent Ideal Novelty & Toy Co, Made in USA". Ideal, circa 1939. Excellent condition except tip of one horn worn. $300/400

354. "Mr. Peanuts" Wooden Doll
9" (23 cm.) All-wooden doll with peanut shaped torso and head, painted features with monocle, wooden-segmented limbs, blue wooden top hat labeled "Mr. Peanuts", baton. Circa 1940 for Planters Peanut Co. Excellent condition. $300/400

355. "Jiminy Cricket" by Ideal
8" (20 cm.) All wooden doll with egg-shaped head, painted side-glancing eyes, carved mouth, wooden top hat, wooden torso, all-wooden segmented limbs and tail, white glove hands, blue shoes, with red wooden umbrella, cloth collar and hat brim. Marked "Jiminy Cricket, des.& c. by Walt Disney. Made by Ideal Novelty & Toy Co, Long Island NY." Excellent condition. Circa 1940. $500/700

356. "Mortimer Snerd" by Ideal
12" (31 cm.) Composition head depicting radio show star, red hair, elongated nose, goofy smile with two teeth, wooden torso, wire flexible arms and legs, composition hands, wooden feet, original cloth costume. Marked "Ideal Doll Made in USA", designed by Joseph Kallus for Ideal, circa 1939. $300/400